Reviews for *18 Steps to an All-Star LinkedIn Profile*

Working with Andrea motivated me, she actually made me a social media practitioner. I love it.

18 Steps to an All-Star LinkedIn Profile is truthful, simple, and efficient. It makes it easy to get started.

The book translates Andrea's energy and passion for people through social media, as she is willing to make any one of us shine in our own ways.

Julian Kasparian
CEO, BNP Paribas Securities Services, Hong Kong

Andrea is my digital angel. She opened my eyes to the possibility of LinkedIn and more broadly to social media, showing me the huge potential for business professionals. When it comes to understanding how to use LinkedIn with integrity and power, Andrea Edwards and *18 Steps* should be your first port of call.

Stanimira Koleva
EVP, International Markets, Sage Software

Andrea is leading the digital battle of good against mediocre when it comes to social leadership. This is the starting point everyone needs to just get done, because from here, you'll start to see the true power social leadership brings, not just to yourself, but to your business. Andrea has been a key partner in this transformation for my company. I suggest you listen to her.

Nishan Weerasinghe
CMO, Fortune 500 MNC, Asia Top 50 Marketer

Andrea is totally passionate about the business and personal benefits of social leadership. She has been a leader in this space for many years and has kept up and refined her approach as the industry has changed. I have seen her share her advice and inspire groups with her energy for the subject.

The advice she shares in *18 Steps to an All-Star LinkedIn Profile* is simple to put in place yet highly effective and recommended if you want to see business results.

Michelle Cockrill
Head of Marketing and Communications,
BNP Paribas Securities Services APAC

Andrea's ability to break down how to get started on your social leadership journey is outstanding. I've shared variations of this information across my internal and external networks more times than I can count. Andrea's passion for social leadership and her ability to relate the results to business outcomes is what motivates many people I know to finally get started. But more than that, they believe it's worth the time to invest in creating value—not noise—across their own networks. Thank you for continuing to lead and inspire all of us to do differently.

Wendy McEwan
Marketing and Business Executive working across Asia

I know when I first started on social media, it was photos of what I ate and where I was. My friends were the same. As time moved on, I observed connections who were able to position themselves as someone to listen to; they had something important to share and were very clear on who they were, personally and in business. So, I asked myself, how does that picture of a coffee or odd-looking cat jump that ravine and become something of importance to other people?

Andrea's book, *18 Steps to an All-Star LinkedIn Profile* showed me. Andrea has eloquently and without fuss taken away the fear and loathing from putting yourself out there and making

YOURSELF the brand. Her step-by-step approach is a real-world way to get your voice, brand, and message out there without the "preach."

Sinisa Nikolic
Director, AP Cognitive Systems, Fortune 500 MNC

Andrea has written a must-read primer for anyone taking their first step towards creating a brand for themselves on LinkedIn. As my first guide in this regard, Andrea, her workshop, and 18 Steps definitely set me on the right track on my personal branding journey. Read this book—and learn from one of the best.

Thariyan Chacko
Group Manager, Microsoft

There are many people advising you to be more active on LinkedIn, but very few tell you how to be more active and why. This book—in 18 steps—will help you kick-start your journey on LinkedIn and provides honest guidance on how you can share your true passion, unleashing the digital leader in you. If you have a lot of knowledge or are passionate to make a positive impact in the world, then start here.

Deepthi Anne
Co-founder of Tech Athena Solution Architect, Fortune 500 MNC

What I love most about Andrea Edwards' timely book is that it provides executives, managers, and thought leaders with a step-by-step guide on how to succeed using LinkedIn while at the same time ensuring that quality and integrity are central to your social media strategy. A much-needed handbook which will help you cut through the noise and make a bigger impact in the world. Highly recommended.

James Taylor MBA FR5A
Keynote Speaker on Business Creativity,
Innovation and Artificial Intelligence

Why do I need to learn it and *who* do I need to learn it from? These are two questions I ask myself when choosing what to read or study. Having an effective LinkedIn profile is going to help you sell yourself, influence your stakeholders, and have conversations with people you would never normally be able to reach. I know this because I've done it, and the person that "kicked my butt" to get it done was Andrea Edwards. There's no better thought leader when it comes to digital conversations and social media.

Andrew Bryant, CSP
Author, *Self Leadership*

Andrea's book got me in the first sentence. "What is social leadership? It's you!" Wow. Straight to the point. Her writing style pulls no punches, and it sets the direction of her very practical and insights-driven approach on how and why social leadership is so important, and, more importantly, HOW to do it on the world's biggest professional platform. A must-read for anyone serious about being heard and seen and making a difference in this beautiful, chaotic world we call home.

Natalie Turner
Author, *Yes, You Can Innovate*, Inventor of the Six 'I's of Innovation.

Everyone talks about LinkedIn but here is your chance to truly do it well by reading *18 Steps* and putting it into action. Andrea provides a powerful approach to LinkedIn that every executive should use to get ahead. Get started now and let your brand stand out!

Jerome Joseph, CSP
Author, *The Brand Playbook*, Global Speaker and Brand Strategist

There are many people who profess that they are social media specialists, yet they don't practice what they preach. If you're looking for a person that is the best in the business and who walks the talk, then Andrea Edwards, the Digital Conversationalist, is the person you need to learn from.

In her new book, *18 Steps to an All-Star LinkedIn Profile*, Andrea walks the reader through the ins and outs of why you need to be on social media and then teaches you step-by-step what you need to do—and how—to create an impactful profile.

If you've never met Andrea, I can tell you she's the real deal.

Pamela Wigglesworth
CEO, Experiential Hands-on Learning, Author,
The 50-60 Something Start-up Entrepreneur

I remember Andrea stating to me and others: *never outsource your voice.* This stuck with me, and I fired my social media manager. If anyone I know understands social media, it is Andrea. She thoroughly gets what it takes to build a great social media presence, especially on LinkedIn. In *18 Steps,* she gives an outright, honest, no-nonsense account of the steps to take on how to make the most of LinkedIn—especially if you're a beginner!

She is my social media guru. Why? Because she debunks the LinkedIn myths and doesn't fluff it up. She beautifully tells it how it is, and in a super generous way. I recommend you read this transforming book today. It will change your view of LinkedIn and, most of all, how to gain from this B2B platform. Don't outsource your voice, insource it.

Kevin Cottam
Author, *The Nomadic Mindset*

Andrea unplugs social media and takes a deep dive into the importance of understanding its relevance when building relationships both internally and externally for business. One read of this gem will set leaders and employees on a journey of personal empowerment that will certainly impact their long-term professional fulfillment.

John Gordon
CEO, Expat Choice, Asia

LinkedIn is such an essential tool in business today and having an all-star LinkedIn profile is essential if you want to stand out from the crowd and do business with just the right people. Andrea Edwards, the Digital Conversationalist, has written the ultimate guide to creating that perfect profile in *18 Steps*. She gives practical, step-by-step tips on how to improve your profile to enable you to shine. I've already gone and given my page on LinkedIn a tune-up following Andrea's insights.

Lindsay Adams
The Relationships Guy

Andrea Edwards is THE guru of LinkedIn. Her extensive experience helps clearly convey the essentials needed to become a real STAR on LinkedIn. This book is all you need to get started.

What I find most appealing about Andrea Edwards is her down-to-earth way of writing, her unflagging determination to help people get over their hesitancy online so they discover their unique talents and gifts, and to support them in getting their voices out into the world. Andrea's book will help you get your message to work.

We can all change the world for the better, just like Andrea. Read this and get started...

Cathy Johnson
The Authenticity Coach

18 Steps to an All-Star LinkedIn Profile is packed with practical gems that will help you elevate your personal brand. Andrea leads powerfully by example and brings tremendous clarity to the process of developing social leadership. This book is your personal coach, inspiring you to take action. Highly recommended!

Karen Leong
Author, *Win People Over*, Founding Director of Influence Solutions

Social media can be confusing, particularly for senior management teams. How can you show authenticity, be true to your corporate brand, and continue to add value? Too often social media is treated like a free space for adverts! Andrea Edwards has the experience and credibility to show you what actually works.

Andrea continues to embody what is needed on social media and in particular, LinkedIn. Professional and personal positioning with the Goldilocks approach—not too little, not too much, but just right. Using Andrea's advice as mapped out in this book will put you well ahead of your competition and, to be frank, you would be crazy not to buy this book and follow it religiously.

Warwick Merry, CSP
Master Success Speaker and MC

This book is simply brilliant. Andrea shares important, practical information in an easy-to-read manner—with glimpses of her wonderful sense of humor and passion for leading sustainable, positive change. It's simple, essential, and easy to implement as you read through—in a style relevant to you and your industry. If you want to be a great connector, you need this book!

Kerrie Phipps
Author, *Do Talk to Strangers*

18 STEPS
TO AN ALL-STAR
LinkedIn
PROFILE

HOW TO GET STARTED ON LINKEDIN

ANDREA T EDWARDS

For every book you buy, I plant a tree.

This book is dedicated to my love, Steve Johnson.

When you commit to sharing your life with someone, there's always a lot of give and take.

Agreeing to do that with someone deeply invested in the digital world adds a whole other dimension to marriage.

You're not an "Instagram husband" my love, but I really do appreciate you for being by my side through it all. You're the best of the best xxxxx

Foreword

I remember the first time I heard Andrea speak. It was at an APSS Speaker's convention in Singapore in May 2018.

I was so impressed by her! She had her signature Lichtenstein-esque slides which is still something she uses today. You see those slides, and you KNOW they're Andrea's.

That talk inspired me to make more of my Linkedin presence. I had just walked out on an amazing job and a career that I enjoyed but didn't love. I was starting out as a professional speaker and had no clue how to do it.

There were three things she said that day on that stage that have shaped the way I've approached my Linkedin presence.

The first was what she said in response to a question on automation. She advised us to think about our posts as if we were getting on a stage each time. Would you subcontract that or automate it? Most of us wouldn't onstage, and so we shouldn't online, either. I have never forgotten that and every time I post, I think about getting up on a stage and delivering my message.

The second is about being generous. It's really the secret sauce to genuine connections on Linkedin. Use the opportunity to shine a light on other people and bigger issues. It does not always have to be about us. My most viral Linkedin post to date was not about me but rather was part of the #thislittlegirlisme campaign for Inspiring Girls in the run up to the International Day of the Girl in 2021.

The third was from her opening slide: "There's never been a better time to be awesome on social media. There's never been a worse time to be bad on social media." It was exactly what I needed to hear to put some consistency and creativity behind my presence on the platform.

I heard her talk, I bought the first edition of this book, and I worked through it step-by-step.

You need to put in the effort. Do it straight away. Don't just read without action. I had the book open in front of my laptop as I upgraded my Linkedin presence and I can only recommend that you do the same.

Then start showing up consistently and with purpose. I've seen it time and again, LinkedIn can deliver career and business success for anyone.

Two years after I started applying Andrea's 18 steps, in November 2020, Linkedin named me one of their Top Voices. I've been featured many times on Linkedin News and it's opened so many doors for me.

In all honesty, I'm a terrible salesperson and I manage to be successful as an entrepreneur because I'm good at Linkedin. All my leads are inbound. Every. Single. One. I do no outbound marketing at all.

Clients find me because of Linkedin. And that is because of the Amazing Andrea Edwards who first introduced me to the wonders of Linkedin.

Other people were spending their time on social media. Thanks to Andrea, I learned to invest my time on Linkedin.

I learned from this book and you can too!

Your work cannot speak for itself. You need to be the most vocal advocate for your work. LinkedIn makes that easy to do. You just have to learn how. That's why this book is in your hands.

Andrea is a Linkedin legend who has created rockstars on this platform. This book is her step-by-step guide to building your profile, establishing your network, and sharing content. It's over to you now. What will you do with this gift?

Lavinia Thanapathy
LinkedIn Top Voice

Why Social Leadership?

It's you... **Amplified!**

It's what you stand for. What you believe in.

It's how you think and act.

It is the packaging up of all of you, which you then actively and passionately share with the world online, driven by a goal of creating change—in mindset, behavior or better ways of doing things.

We can all be social leaders today. We all have the power to make a positive difference in the world, we just need to step into it and claim our space in the digital world.

In fact, if you have something valuable to offer and are not joining the global conversation, are you doing humanity a disservice by not contributing your message? Are you absconding your obligation to your fellow humans and all life on earth?

If you are intelligent, passionate, caring, and have a solution for the challenges our world faces, or are willing to step up and support others who do, then it's time to join the conversation. We need you. No more excuses for your absence.

It is time to claim your digital voice as a social leader. Because in today's digital and physical world, **when we own our voice, we own our future!**

@AndreaTEdwards

Contents

A Quick Introduction to Social Leadership

What I Know to be True

Building a strong, powerful social leadership position and really owning your voice is how you build your future. Whatever you want to do, whatever you hope to achieve, whatever path you have mapped out for your life, you can get there by connecting to others on social media. You do this by intelligently participating, with deep integrity, with a mindset of service in community conversations. By building your social leadership presence, you cement yourself as an expert in your field. You become the go-to person, the master of your domain.

In a world undergoing cataclysmic change across all aspects of life, we must consider our social media presence as one of the most important career-building tools at our disposal today. It's also an opportunity to contribute to great social change. From a professional perspective, think of it as health insurance for your career. However, YOU must embrace it and get started. No one will do this for you. It's your voice, and only you can best represent you.

Still, there are not enough professionals taking their social leadership presence seriously, and the way people interact with social media is rapidly changing. As social media takes an ever more central place in our collective political, economic, and emotional lives, the only way to avoid being left behind is to establish your presence early and cultivate it with agility and sensitivity to evolving trends.

Not only can social leadership dramatically change your career path, personal opportunities, and profile, but it will also build and change your business—or the business you work for—in such fundamental ways. You'll wonder why you waited! This is happening—now.

Employee advocacy is a hot topic these days and your employer will expect you to build your profile soon if they haven't asked you already. Take control by getting out in front, without buying into the current employee advocacy message. Own your social leadership. Employee advocacy is about the company you work for. Social leadership is about you, with benefits to your employer as a happy, symbiotic secondary effect. This is a very important distinction.

It comes down to this: don't allow the company you work for to control your profile. Your profile is yours, and you shouldn't delegate or outsource it to anyone. There is enough noise out there, and the majority of current employee advocacy programs are highly ineffective. Sure, get help if you need it, but be the voice behind your message.

It's time for all of us to step up and become social leaders, with a mindset of serving our audience in a meaningful and authentic way. You can only achieve this by participating and getting your hands dirty. You can't understand social media or gauge its value from the outside, looking in. If you outsource your voice, you are seeing none of the value that active participation delivers. It's a big miss.

Only true engagement by listening, participating, and leading—on the relevant platforms used daily by your audience—will unlock those insights and allow you to have a meaningful impact.

Important takeaways:

1. It's not scary or hard. You don't need to invest huge amounts of time.

2. It's all about the quality of content you create and/or share.

3. Getting focused is the most critical part of being successful.

4. It's about creating a habit of giving to and serving your community by sharing knowledge that can change lives and businesses. A social leader understands it's not about self-promotion, but about giving value to their audience.

Social leadership, quite simply, is an act of service.

McKinsey's 2013 report nearly a decade ago found that any company that develops a critical mass of leaders who master the skills of social media will experience significant business benefits. This is as true today as it was in 2013. Yet still, it's not dealt with in the right way.

Here are some of those business benefits according to McKinsey, along with my own edits and additions.[1] You will:

-   Become more creative, innovative, and agile

-   Attract and retain the best talent

-   Tap deeper into the capabilities and ideas of employees and stakeholders

---

1   "Six social-media skills every leader needs," McKinsey Quarterly, Roland Deiser and Sylvain Newton, February 2013.

- Become more effective at collaborating across internal and external boundaries

- Enjoy a higher degree of global integration, which is critical for the future of borderless business

- Create more loyal customer relationships, leading to greater brand equity

- Play an industry leadership role by leveraging partners to co-create, co-develop, and collaborate

- Be more likely to create new business models that capitalize on the potential of evolving communication technologies

- Empower your business to confront the shortcomings of traditional organizational design

- Address shortcomings to develop infrastructure that underpins strategic use of social technologies

- Initiate a positive loop, allowing individuals and businesses to capitalize on the opportunities and disruptions that come with the community of a networked society. Gain the rewards of new a competitive advantage.

Considering this paper was published in 2013, and that the benefits of a critical mass of leaders embracing social media are phenomenal, it's surprising to still see so few leaders and businesses really engaging in social leadership as a transformational strategy for their companies, especially as we move forward into the unique challenges of the 2020s.

Today more than ever, it's critical for all employees to be engaged socially, keeping their profile alive in times of separation. Social leadership delivers the humanity of any business, through the voice of its people.

The Benefits are Enormous—for You and Your Business

Adopting a social leadership presence will change the way you think. It will change the way you work. When it becomes a strategic priority for your business, it will harness the voice of your team members to transform your business from the inside out. It creates a people-focused culture that benefits everyone within your community. It is the core tool of innovation in business today because it is about communication—the essence of being human.

A social leadership culture breaks down hierarchies and silos. It positions all employees as externally focused (rather than the internal focus so common in corporate culture) and it empowers all employees in a business—not just those at the very top. If you want to build trust, social leadership opens that door.

Overstating it? I am not.

I had the privilege of working with IBM across the Asia Pacific for a number of years. We have a full 24-month track record demonstrating business value and employee wins.

This data is based on interviews and responses from a survey of 100 IBM employees who participated in my social leadership training. This is shared, with IBM's authorization. For more see the full case study published with IBM.[2]

This is their view on what happened when they made social leadership a priority.

- Pipeline generated directly from social media in the first year was minimum of US$57 million followed by US$140 million in the second year. This is 145% growth.

- Wins in the first year were minimum of US$24 million. In the second year it went up to US$40 million, which is 66% growth.

The top five benefits highlighted by employees:

1. Clients learning about IBM from the content I am sharing: 54%

2. Growing belief in the effectiveness of strategic social selling: 52%

3. I am learning more as I create content and actively seek world-class content to share with my networks: 49%

4. Bigger networks globally, opening doors to opportunities for IBM and myself: 48%

5. Believe IBM is on the right track as a business of the future: 38%

Was all the above hard to achieve? No. They began with these 18 steps.

The thing I hear from professionals and C-suite leaders all the time is that they want to do it, but they want to do it

---

2 https://www.slideshare.net/AndreaTEdwards/success-story-unleash-your-employees-disrupt-from-within-grow-your-business-103390123

well. They don't want to look foolish or out of step with social media's rapidly changing technologies and culture.

In working with IBM and other multinational organizations, I hear these challenges repeated often. I'm sharing so you, as a leader, can address them.

Six Key Challenges that Hold Employees Back from Social Leadership:

1. Self-confidence: "Why would anyone care what I have to say?"

2. Employees cannot see the benefit to themselves personally—they are happy with their career path as it is.

3. Time commitment is a barrier, even with simple steps identified, such as posting one article per week that's aligned to your focus on LinkedIn.

4. Managers are not embracing social leadership and employees lack support. Leadership buy-in is critical.

5. Perceived as a waste of time by peers who have not embraced social leadership—employees struggle with feeling this work is not valued. It's a culture change that starts from the top.

6. Many employees struggle with the idea that successful social leadership requires more long-term engagement and persistence than they can commit to.

It all starts with getting the tools you need in place and then getting focused. This book is about helping you organize your presence on LinkedIn, the world's biggest online professional network, and it's a starting point. Simple, easy steps you can easily do. Most people are stuck—at the beginning. If this is you, stick with me through these pages and I will help you move past this common barrier to getting started, setting you up to thrive in the social leadership age.

Social media is more than a LinkedIn profile or a Facebook page. It's more than your friends' lunchtime foodie posts, where they're hanging out right now, what they're doing as they post yet another selfie, those annoying motivational memes, or whatever irks you about social media—and there's plenty that's irksome!

What it provides us with is an opportunity to openly communicate a focused message with our communities and a platform to have discussions with like-minded people. When we do this well on LinkedIn, we change how we do business— and we can even change the world.

The transformative power of social media and content marketing comes into play when it is embraced from the very top of an organization—and then right across it. It is only when every CEO genuinely engages as a social leader and empowers every employee to do the same, that we will see a fundamental shift in how we do business and how we run our organizations. This shift will make businesses and organizations more successful, more open, and more trusted.

It is time for us all to lead socially, to be more authentic, more passionate, and more giving. It is time to open ourselves up, to be vulnerable, to smash down unhelpful hierarchies, and to knock down the PR walls executives have been hiding behind for decades. It is time to join the digital arena because that's the only place where we can fully understand today's consumers and grow our organizations. It's an age of collaboration, of service, and of engagement, and it's time for you to get out there in the digital world.

If you are reading these words out of a desire to make a change in your life and for your business, whether you're a young professional keen to understand how to build a professional profile to support your career ambitions or a business leader persuaded that your organization can become something more through the power of social media and online content, this book is for you. What we'll get to here is the stuff that is the starting point for real business transformation today.

This book is just the starting point. Enjoy the journey with me and put any cynicism in your back pocket, for now. All I ask is that you give me a chance to change your mind—and hopefully inspire you, too.

When initially I wrote *18 Steps*, I planned to write *The Social Leadership Manifesto* next. This would take you deeper into the strategies and tactics that ensure you are a social leader your industry pays attention to. I've included an extract for you at the end of this book.

Instead, as the pandemic closed in, I realized something different was needed in the world, which is why I wrote *Uncommon Courage: an Invitation*. It's a book designed to help each of us look within and do the work, so that we can become the best version of ourselves. Social leadership is a part of the message. As are these topics:

- Self-awareness
- Self-empowerment

- Empower others
- External influence
- Career thoughts
- Climate courage

If you've struggled through the past few years, *Uncommon Courage* is written to give you a boost and to help manage the chaos of the decade of disruption—the 2020s.

But first, let's start with the basics and get your LinkedIn profile looking world-class.

Cheers, Andrea

A Few Introductory Thoughts on LinkedIn

Pick Your
Platform

Where do you need to be present on social media to build your professional career? Like all things to do with social media, there is no single answer. When working with professionals across all industries, I say to prioritize LinkedIn first, then Twitter, but TikTok has certainly gained a place of relevance for many professionals. It all depends on *your* audience. The statistics are clear: while they are far from the only choices, LinkedIn and Twitter are generally the professional social platforms of choice for business.

The best place to start is to research social media use in your industry. Ask around if you don't know. Identify your industry leaders. See which platforms they are active on, and you'll have your answer. If you're in an industry slow to embrace social media and you can't find much presence, you have a unique pioneering opportunity to establish the priority social channels for your sector.

Perhaps you are in a creative industry, or maybe you are an educator, a doctor, or a charity worker. The most important question to ask, depending on what you do and what you want to achieve is this: where is everyone else in your industry? If you're in the visual industry, Instagram and TikTok are superb. Facebook is also a critical social media platform to be part of, given its scale.

Of course, there may be platforms or ways of using social media that are unique to your country, language, or industry. Examples include WeChat, Weibo, and Line. Or perhaps you will find your leadership opportunity in a more private corner of the internet. Business leaders often set up private, invitation-only communities on LinkedIn, for example. How do you get that invitation? Do you know who owns the group? Does someone in your network belong to it, and can they help you get an invite? The more you build your profile and professional presence, the more invitations you will receive to network and join relevant conversations.

Some industries, such as energy and construction, operate almost exclusively within LinkedIn Groups, as another example of use. Deals are done in these groups, RFPs are shared. Does your industry work that way? Ask around to find out.

The way the major platforms are used varies not only by industry but across different countries. For example, Facebook has a very different role in Indonesia, Thailand, and the Philippines compared to Singapore, Australia, and Hong Kong. For the latter three, it's more focused on family and community than business. The former three use it a lot for business, and messenger is a HUGE part of that. Depending on where you operate, you may need to make Facebook a bigger business priority. Understanding what works in each local market is critical.

Another critical question is where and how you enjoy participating on social media. If you don't enjoy your chosen social media platform, you will never participate with the same passion as you would on a platform you love.

If you're a business professional who loves Instagram or TikTok, these will be powerful places for you to build your presence. Look at what other professionals are doing on these platforms to seek inspiration. The most important thing is that you love what you're doing.

It's very important to actually enjoy the platform(s) you are on. As an example, TikTok has zero appeal to me. This doesn't mean I'll ignore it, but I'm not desperate to give it a go, either. It just doesn't seem to suit my personality. This is important!

For me professionally, it's LinkedIn, Twitter, Facebook, Instagram (although more personal), and YouTube. What's in the mix of your ideal social media cocktail?

If, on the other hand, you're barely participating anywhere and you want to start building your credibility as a social leader, you must start with LinkedIn, the international business platform.

If you haven't done it yet, it's well past time to move beyond the old thinking that LinkedIn is just for recruitment. Just so you know, LinkedIn gets 15 times more impressions for content shared than it does for job postings, a number that's only going up. It's a content platform first.

No question, LinkedIn is an enormously influential platform with world-class content and unparalleled networking opportunities. When you find yourself checking LinkedIn on the weekend, as you do other social media, you'll know it has come into its own as a powerful information resource that will help you flourish in your career and industry.

However, for everyone who complains that LinkedIn is flooded with nonsense, I'll point out a fundamental truth of social media: LinkedIn, like any platform, is only as good as you make it. Invest in it. Create and share quality content. Unfollow people or businesses that are not delivering value to you. Over time it will become a powerful resource that will help you be successful and establish your eminence.

We Are All
Responsible for
LinkedIn

You, me, and over 800 million other users are responsible for the quality of LinkedIn. I believe in taking personal responsibility, and this is as true for social media as for any aspect of life. In the spirit of building a better online world for ourselves, it's important we address upfront the fact that LinkedIn is awesome, but it comes with many annoyances.

We've all read threads by people complaining that members of LinkedIn are making Facebook-like posts on what's supposed to be a professional platform. We've seen attractive women posting alluring pictures that garner thousands of comments running the gamut from "Inappropriate!" to "You're so pretty." Naturally, the people who spend their time writing such comments have no idea how bad it makes them look, and the people posting the pictures are similarly out of touch—if we're even looking at real accounts. It doesn't take much digging to recognize the many fake accounts out there.

Look out for posts from accounts with few followers, little detail, weird credentials or even brand-new accounts require you look closely. All of these, as well as young pretty girls, signify a good chance it's fake and by participating in those posts, you look foolish. Dig deeper always!

Needless to say, if you are new to LinkedIn and getting started, you want to avoid looking like that—and these 18 steps will help you.

Then there's the connection who is proud their kid has graduated from university after a hard slog. This parent is naturally thrilled about their kid's achievement, and some friends are supportive, but the rest of LinkedIn says, "No, not welcome here." Some of our connections will inevitably post cute videos or memes of animals or share their religious or political views, whereby we quickly express our outrage: "Not on LinkedIn, thank you!"

Look out for the new toggle to turn "off" politics. I do not agree with this move by LinkedIn, because if you do not understand the world, how can you be effective in business? However, this book is focused on providing all the updates I'm seeing, and turning off politics is one option.

The posts that concern me the most, though, are people wanting to walk away from LinkedIn because "it's not a good platform anymore." Too much self-promotion. Too much useless information. Too much nonsense. And I agree—there is far too much nonsense on LinkedIn today, but walking away is not the solution. We can and must make it better, together, for all of us.

I believe LinkedIn is an amazing platform, and I have been 100% committed to growing my LinkedIn presence for more than a decade. Yes, there's a lot more nonsense going on, but I've developed the ability to filter out the annoyances outlined above:

Pretty girl: ignore these posts or be entertained by the comments without getting involved. Feisty trolls can break up a dull day!

Pets, politics, and religion: I'm not on LinkedIn for pets or religion. With politics, I'm deeply interested in expert view and the wider geopolitical stories, but I'm not interested in the divisive right/left arguments. For these, I'm not going to react. Connections making such posts are ignored...

The rest: I simply can't be bothered to care. I'm looking for useful information and if you're wasting my time, I'll give my attention (which is, after all, the most valuable currency on social media) to someone whose posts enrich and inform me.

In general, I encourage you not to take it all too seriously. Getting worked up about what bothers you on social media is a waste of your energy. **Let it go, focus on the connections who are delivering great value, and make sure you are focused on being awesome yourself, and on making the conversations you engage in meaningful.** That's something you can do AND you can control. The rest is just noise! Ignore it.

My Suggested Strategy?

Focus on being the best version of yourself on LinkedIn and across all social media. Ask yourself: are you delivering information that will bring value to your audience? Are you celebrating people in your networks by engaging with them or praising them for a job well done? Are you regularly writing someone a recommendation?

In a noisy, chaotic, divided world, we must build stronger filters and blank out the nonsense. If you see someone participating on LinkedIn in a way you think is inappropriate, don't comment—with one click you can remove them from your world. Look for the three dots … at the top right of every post. Clicking on them allows you to unfollow, report, and more. It's very easy. Let them figure out that if they're consistently posting foolishly, their connections start dropping off.

Is your LinkedIn inbox full of sales nonsense and useless outreach? This can make it impossible to keep track of the messages you actually want to read. One approach is to reply and challenge them: "Why did you send this to me? Did you review my profile first?" I can guarantee that 99% of senders will not respond, but you won't get spam from them again, either!

Not that it stops the spam coming in. I rarely even check my LinkedIn inbox these days. I haven't been able to keep up with it for a long time, but the idiotic messages here have made it an unmanageable place. You too? A challenge we must address, but for now, maybe you need to ignore it too?

If you have connections who are participating inappropriately and you know them personally, talk to them. The best way to lead is by example, but some people are stubborn or just lacking in observation skills and awareness of their own impact. Talk to them and help them be better. They won't all hear you, but at least you tried to approach them from an angle of service. You can unfriend as needed.

We really do have a shared responsibility on LinkedIn—and all social media—to make it better. It's not easy. Stuff will continue to drive you nuts but build your filters for looking past the nonsense. If you are a deep thinking, intelligent, passionate, and self-aware person—we need you on LinkedIn. If enough of us can come together and make it a better place, we will all benefit.

Something equally important to me is to be kind, always. There is enough nasty stuff going on in the world right now and personally, I don't differentiate between violent behavior in the "real" world and people ripping each other to shreds on social media. Nastiness is nastiness. We need more givers, not haters if we want to make the world a better place.

LinkedIn has done an amazing job building a world class content platform, and it's only going to keep growing and evolving, but we all have a part to play in its success. That means we must all be focused on being awesome by delivering value to our communities, lifting others up, and using the platform as if it were the best version of itself—a tool to build our dreams and make them come true.

This is powerful stuff.

Why is LinkedIn Important?

Today, LinkedIn is *the* professional platform on social media. It's absolutely critical to understand the many ways you can use it and the features available (on a platform that's always evolving and mostly getting better), as well as how to participate in a meaningful way. Don't underestimate its power, even if you don't admire how other people use it. Don't worry about them—your job is to outshine them.

Reasons to use LinkedIn—let's look at the data as of 2022:

- More than one-third of professionals on the planet are on LinkedIn.

- There are well over 800 million members, with two new members every second.

- To break it down, the North American region is 202 million (180 million in the US), Europe has 198 million, Asia Pacific 206 million, Latin America 114 million, and the Middle East and Africa 39 million. These numbers are constantly growing.

- The Asia Pacific figure may see reductions in the future, following the announcement in 2021 by Microsoft of the closure of LinkedIn China, due to "a considerably more difficult operating environment and higher regulatory requirements."[3] With 55+ million users, this is a significant reduction and important for anyone focusing on China.

- There are 110 industries across 200 countries and territories represented.

- More than 57 million companies are represented on LinkedIn, as well as 120,000 schools. It's getting close to 80% of all users now outside of the US.

- LinkedIn is currently available in 24 languages: Arabic, English, Simplified Chinese, Traditional Chinese, Czech, Danish, Dutch, French, German, Indonesian, Italian, Japanese, Korean, Malay, Norwegian, Polish, Portuguese, Romanian, Russian, Spanish, Swedish, Tagalog, Thai, and Turkish.

- There are more than 30 million students and recent grads on LinkedIn. 30% of millennials are on LinkedIn and more than 200,000 college students join LinkedIn every month.

- The largest age demographic on LinkedIn is 25–34, accounting for 59.9% of users, with 18–24 the second-largest bracket, at 20.3%.[4]

- This is followed by 35–54 at 16.9%, and over 55s account for 3% of total users.[5]

- 57.5% of LinkedIn users are male, 42.6% are female.[6]

3   https://www.linkedin.com/pulse/linkedin-leaving-china-sam-maiyaki/
4   https://datareportal.com/reports/digital-2020-october-global-statshot
5   Hootsuite/We Are Social, https://datareportal.com/reports/digital-2020-october-global-statshot
6   Hootsuite/We Are Social, https://datareportal.com/reports/digital-2020-october-global-statshot

- Key decision-makers make up 65% of LinkedIn members.[7]

- LinkedIn internal data has discovered that engaged employees lead to eight times more company page views, four times more company page followers, seven times more job views, and four times more job applications.[8]

- Google loves LinkedIn. When searching for your name, don't be surprised if your LinkedIn profile is the first suggestion.

According to Influencer Marketing Hub, LinkedIn is the number one choice for professionals to gather to stay connected and informed.[9]

LinkedIn is where the largest number of professionals by far gather to stay connected and informed, advance their careers, and work smarter.

LinkedIn has:

- 46 million B2B decision-makers

- 17 million opinion leaders

- 6 million IT decision-makers

- 40 million mass affluent

- 10 million C-level execs

---

7   https://influencermarketinghub.com/linkedin-stats/
8   https://influencermarketinghub.com/linkedin-stats/
9   https://influencermarketinghub.com/linkedin-stats/

Learn From Those Who Inspire You

To get started, building confidence is important. My suggestion is to make a list of 10 people you admire on LinkedIn (or any social media platform) and review their profiles. Pay attention to how they actively participate. Take notes on what makes them stand out, as well as how they implement the strategies we'll discuss in the following pages. You will stand out if you watch, learn, and listen from the best of what social media has to offer.

Many professionals fail to make time for this simple reflection in advance, which means they are missing an opportunity to think about what makes a powerful online presence *pop*. Spend some time on this exercise and you will be off to an excellent start.

ACTION BOX: My list of 10 professional social media profiles that I admire and want to learn from:

1. _____

2. _____

3. _____

4. _____

5. _____

6. _____

7. _____

8. _____

9. _____

10. _____

Dog-ear This Page
for Later

Before we continue, mark this page to refer back to later as you implement the advice in the following sections. When you start building your LinkedIn profile, it's important to understand character limits, or the number of letters (not words) you can use for each section. Character counts include spaces and all other characters—letters, numbers, symbols, emojis, etc.

If you know the limit upfront, you'll be able to create content tailored to the confines of that space, which will save you time once you're uploading those texts. Try to use the maximum number of characters allowed. It's your story, and there's a lot to tell.

My advice is always to write this content into a document that you save. I have watched many post directly to LinkedIn and lose this content when the platform has those weird moments. Losing your carefully composed 2,000-character "about" section can make grown men cry—I've witnessed it!

To make sure this doesn't happen, set up a social media profile folder on your computer and make sure all updates are written and saved there first.

Character limits for LinkedIn

The information here is correct at the time of writing (always subject to change) and character limits are listed unless minimum is indicated:

- First Name: 20

- Last Name: 40

- Professional Headline (Desktop): 220

- Professional Headline (Mobile): 240

- About section, previously called professional summary: 2,600

- Interests: 1,000

- Vanity URL (the personalization of your LinkedIn address): 5–30, after "www.linkedin.com/in/"

- Website URL: 256—this is your website address outside LinkedIn

- Skills: 50 skills with 80 characters per skill

- Position Title: 100

- Position Description: 200 characters minimum, 2,000 characters maximum

- Profile Publication Title: 255

- Profile Publication Description: 2,000

- Recommendation: 3,000

- Additional Info/Advice for Contacting: 2,000

- Phone number: 25

- Instant Message: 25

- Address: 1,000

- Probably the biggest change, since the first edition of this book, is to LinkedIn status updates. A status update is the post you write on LinkedIn. It is now 3,000 characters; with the first 200 characters visible and the rest hidden until you click the **see more** button. Previously it was only 700 characters, so you can now say significantly more.

Creating text with these limits in mind will save you time later, I promise. You can also use this text for other social media platforms. For example, my professional headline on LinkedIn is used for Twitter.

For all the latest information on LinkedIn, check out the LinkedIn help page.[10] Ask questions and hopefully, you'll get your answers.

ACTION BOX: Drafting my 120 characters

Experiment here:

1. _____

   _____

2. _____

   _____

3. _____

   _____

---

10 https:// www.linkedin.com/ help/ linkedin

Know Your Social
Selling Index (SSI)

LinkedIn has the Social Selling Index (SSI), which measures the key elements of successful LinkedIn participation.

Before updating your LinkedIn profile, I suggest you start with your SSI. It's important to know where your ranking is on the platform, and it will give you a sense of achievement as you see this number increase.

LinkedIn tracks four key metrics to help you see how effective you are: 1) establish your professional brand, 2) find the right people, 3) engage with insights, and 4) build relationships. These four categories combine to make your Social Selling Index.

How Do You Find It?

Open a new window and type www.linkedin.com/sales/ssi into the URL bar. Because this is a separate page, you won't be able to access it through your LinkedIn profile. You, however, will need to log on to LinkedIn to see your result, which means you need to have your password handy.

Here is a recent screenshot of my SSI with a rating of 82, which puts me in the 1% of my network. Considering what I do, I seek to be well over 80, but as we've recently had the holiday season, and I'm dealing with pandemic exhaustion like everyone else, it's a bit lower than normal. Still, I'm in the top 1% for both my industry and network—which means I'm being compared to my actual connections on LinkedIn.

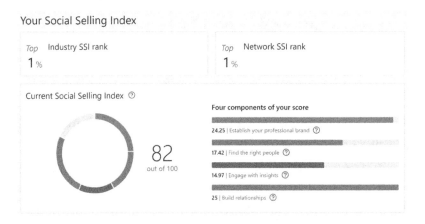

Figure 1. Social Selling Dashboard

Regardless of your role, make it your goal to get to and maintain a minimum SSI of 60. If you're in sales, it should be well over 80. SSI scores between two and four are surprisingly common, and I have seen SSI ratings of zero. (I don't know how one can even *have* a LinkedIn profile and be at zero, but trust me, it's possible!)

Don't worry where you are right now; just work to get it well over 60 as quickly as you can. Following the advice in this book will help you make a huge leap, so commit to getting your SSI score up and then keep it high, through consistent participation across the four areas it measures.

> **ACTION BOX: SSI GOAL #1** _____
>
> by what date ___/___/20___

Your SSI measures four ways in which you can use LinkedIn to achieve professional success:

1. Establish your professional brand (which we'll discuss below)

2. Find the right people

3. Engage with insights

4. Build relationships.

When building your presence on LinkedIn, these four areas are great places to focus your energy to ensure you are building a strong brand the right way. When you go to the SSI page, each of these categories has an explanation, so you can learn more about how to get strong in all four categories.

With that said, sometimes you can do everything right and the number still doesn't change. My nemesis has always been Number 3, engage with insights. I don't know how much more engaged I can be! So, my recommendation is to use it as a guide to get started and if you're intelligently participating by sharing awesome information (your own and content from others) and engaging in posts others share, then you're on the right track.

The essential first step to creating an all-star LinkedIn profile is easy: fill in your profile as completely as possible and keep it updated. Nothing should be static today. If you do everything I suggest here, you can expect your SSI to skyrocket after completing just these steps.

I work with multinationals, ranging from tech companies to banks and logistics companies, where the vast majority of professionals are within the SSI range of 20 to 40 when we start working together. Multinationals are finally focusing on employee advocacy, and the emphasis is definitely LinkedIn. Being a social leader as a business professional—no matter your role in your organization—will be critical for your future. It will be expected. So, get ahead of the curve and start raising your SSI score to a minimum of 60. Your company will soon be measuring this if they aren't already.

An important note. If you are not seeing strong growth of your SSI and are posting to LinkedIn from another platform (Hootsuite, Buffer, Socialoomph, or any other employee engagement platform, etc.) this will impact your result. Post directly to LinkedIn if you want to see and maintain strong growth.

The next three steps require more consistent effort.

Find the Right
People

Here is a chance to address an often-asked question: *should I connect on LinkedIn with people I haven't met before?* And my answer is yes. In the old days of LinkedIn, we were encouraged to only connect with people we had met in real life. However, to become a powerful social leader, you need to network with professionals outside your first-degree connections. That's one reason to do it.

Now, there will always be people you connect with who spam you immediately. Fortunately, it has never been easier to *unfollow* someone on LinkedIn. If you're a woman, you may also get men connecting to tell you how beautiful you are and asking if you are open to having a relationship. It's not Tinder, but some people missed that message. There are also bots on LinkedIn.

My advice is to be selective. Establish rules—such as:

- Only connect with people who have 10 or more con-nections in common with me. Make it 20 connections if you want to be sure.

- They must be connected to someone you know and value

- They must be in your industry, with a certain title

- They must have a profile photo

You can set rules as a preference in your settings.

However, to become a social leader, your goal should be open to connecting with your entire industry and to get beyond your immediate network, because that is how you become a powerful social leader. You may not have personally met everyone face-to-face yet, but you can start building relationships across your industry with LinkedIn today.

With this in mind, I encourage you to connect with people you have not met before in person, but who are aligned with your career. Who knows which of them may be a future employer or employee, or someone who will learn from you and promote your work? The stranger who sends you a request may have heard you speak and been inspired by your words. You won't know if you don't connect.

Twitter used to be the only platform that gave you a global audience well beyond your direct network. It provided a platform to connect with the international thought-leaders in your field. Today, if you intelligently build your network on LinkedIn, you can grow a powerful community interested in what you have to say. Connect with everyone you know, but make sure you stay open to other great connection opportunities.

My rules for connecting with people are:

(Draft them, you can refine them over time)

1. _____

   _____

2. _____

   _____

3. _____

   _____

Note: when you are first-degree connections with someone, they get access to all your contact information. That's why it's important to be a little bit selective. Thankfully it's easier than ever to unfollow people on LinkedIn too.

Engaging or actively participating is what really matters when building a powerful social leadership presence—and increasing your SSI score over the long haul. Talk to people. Comment on what others share. Tag people in the content you share (to tag: simply put @ and then type their name).

Contrary to the way many people use it, LinkedIn is not a megaphone for your views and ideas. It's not a platform to tell people what you're doing and how successful you are at it. Most participants on LinkedIn don't mind a little bit of self-promotion, but if that's all you do, you're missing the *real* opportunity.

LinkedIn is a platform to build relationships and a community.

You can't do this if you're treating it as a one-way street. Build community. Support people, you admire and get involved in conversations. Comment on posts. Share great content. Participate. Encourage. This is what LinkedIn is really all about.

The SSI measurement categories, far from being meaningless statistics, assess how you align with LinkedIn's core values: connecting, engaging, adding value, and building a powerful community.

How Do You Compare with Your Peers?

Look at your network and industry average to find out. This useful SSI metric, found by scrolling down on your SSI page, shows the average score in your network and industry. Make it a goal to consistently exceed this average. SSI averages can vary wildly between industries. My network's average is relatively high (yes, 50 is high!) because I'm connected to a lot of people like me. However, in the marketing/advertising industry, the average sits at around 26—a number that hasn't changed since I first published this book, and it continues to be a figure I find surprising. Leaders in this industry, in particular, should have mastery of all platforms, given that you can only really understand social media if you participate fully in it. Marketing and advertising people, get to work!

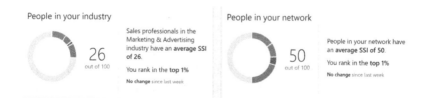

Figure 2. Example of an average SSI

Equally amazing is that social selling skills continue to be abysmally low across all industries, with estimates suggesting less than 30 percent of businesses prioritize social selling. The SSI index will become a job criteria and recruitment factor for sales professionals. Why? Because internal research at large global companies back the claim that leaders with higher SSI scores get better sales results. **If you're in sales or business development, it's time to take SSI very, very seriously.**

According to LinkedIn, social selling leaders get better results:[11]

1. **They create 45% more opportunities than peers with lower SSI**

2. **They are 51% more likely to reach quota**

3. **78% of social sellers outsell peers who don't use social media**

And you need to do this now—before your company sets a minimum SSI requirement for your role! I struggle to understand why professionals will only act when they are required to by their company. The personal career benefits of being a social leader should be enough of an incentive.

> **SSI GOAL #2: Be above my industry average.**
>
> My target is: _____

Stay ahead of the curve on SSI requirements. Get on board and own your voice. Deliver value to your audience and your career will fly!

---

11 https://business.linkedin.com/sales-solutions/social-selling/the-social-selling-index-ssi

When you enter editing mode in the experience section, ensure the **share with network button** is turned **OFF** if you don't want everyone knowing about small updates. Turn **ON** when you're announcing a significant change.

Add experience

Figure 3. Turn off *Notify network* before you update

This is what you'll see when you click on *edit experience* (it's now at the top). The on/off toggle moves sometimes, so keep an eye out for it. It will be grey when off and green when on. Just make sure you slide the toggle **off** for basic updates and turn it back on for significant changes in your career.

It's great to alert your network when you are starting a new position, or once in a while when something significant happens, but you don't want everyone in your network getting a notification every time you tweak your profile.

I once forgot to turn this toggle off when changing my role from Asia-Pacific to Asia. Before I knew it, I had 100 congratulatory messages on the new job that wasn't new. Facepalm! I also forgot to turn it ON when I launched The Digital Conversationalist, which was a big, missed opportunity to raise awareness of my new brand!

Why These 18 Steps, Why Now?

For nearly a decade, I've run my social leadership course with professionals working for the world's largest companies. I love this work and the content herein—which I've handed out to attendees of every training session—remains relevant.

Many of the professionals I've worked with were at zero when it came to where to start on LinkedIn, and so I put together these critical steps to ensure attendees had the basics in hand to get their LinkedIn presence up to date and looking great, along with critical guidance on what matters from the outset.

It's important to get this part of the process done and dusted before moving on to the next phase—building a powerful presence as a social leader, with integrity, a mindset of service, authentic participation, and meaningful intention behind your voice. These 18 steps will provide the guidance you need to get the basics done and get your career and business moving.

What I've written here is the foundation for a great-looking profile, and this is important. Anyone active on LinkedIn will not take you seriously until you get the basics right, so make it a priority.

LinkedIn is in a state of never-ending evolution, to ensure it delivers excellent experiences for us, the users. I've gone wide and deep to capture the changes that matter for you.

If you don't already have a LinkedIn profile, it's time to set one up. If you do have one, make sure you fill in all the sections relevant to you. Here is the basic information you need to get started.

To check the contact information you have already, click on your profile, and below your name, you will see contact info in blue. Click on *contact info* and make sure you've included all the information you want to have available for your contacts. Remember first connections see this information, so it's also why our emails and phones get spammed.

Andrea T. Edwards, CSP 🔊

Inspiring leaders to own their voice with integrity and #UncommonCourage - a committed voice for a better future for all life on earth

Talks about #courage, #climatecrisis, #employeeadvocacy, #knowledgeeconomy, and #socialleadership

Singapore · **Contact info**

Figure 4. Example of the top section of a profile

Here is a checklist so that you can track your way through the basic information in your profile.

❏ **Name**

❏ **Professional profile:** We'll talk about this in more detail later. Just let your current role be your professional title for now, and it will be populated automatically if you don't write an original one.

❏ **Previous positions:** Fill in as much information as you can. If you have big gaps that's OK, but you should explain them so readers aren't left to their own imagination. For example, you can list travel or parenting duties to explain gaps in your work history.

❏ **Education:** Fill it in as far back as you want to go, but I don't recommend including high school unless you are still in high school or have recently graduated.

❏ **Email:** You must provide an email address for your LinkedIn profile, but remember, it's visible to anyone you connect with. I recommend using a personal email, versus a company email, as you never know when you will move on. However, if your company pays for LinkedIn Navigator or other LinkedIn services, you may need to use your company address while in their employment.

❏ **Instant messenger, phone number, and address:** Add these if you want to. But remember, they are visible to connections. I don't include my phone number or address.

❏ **Twitter handle:** What's a handle? It's your address on Twitter or Instagram. My handle, for example, is @AndreaTEdwards. If you don't have one yet, remember to go back to LinkedIn and update it later. Your Twitter handle is critical if you blog on LinkedIn; it automatically includes your handle in tweets when other people share your blogs from LinkedIn.

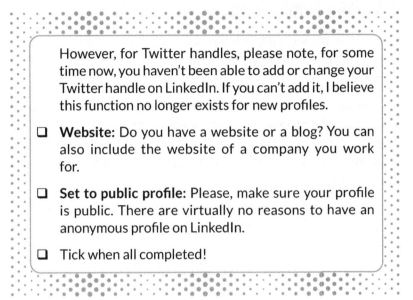

However, for Twitter handles, please note, for some time now, you haven't been able to add or change your Twitter handle on LinkedIn. If you can't add it, I believe this function no longer exists for new profiles.

❑ **Website:** Do you have a website or a blog? You can also include the website of a company you work for.

❑ **Set to public profile:** Please, make sure your profile is public. There are virtually no reasons to have an anonymous profile on LinkedIn.

❑ Tick when all completed!

To get to *edit visibility*, when you are on your profile page, look for this in the top right column.

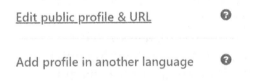

Edit public profile & URL   ❓

Add profile in another language   ❓

Figure 5. Look for this to edit your profile

Click on *edit public profile & URL.*

When a new window opens, in the right-hand column, look for *edit visibility*. Your profile's public visibility should be on and green.

◎ **Edit Visibility**

You control your profile's appearance for people who are not signed in to LinkedIn. The limits you set here affect how your profile appears on search engines, profile badges, and permitted services like Outlook.

Learn more

Your profile's public visibility   On

Figure 6. Turn this to green when you are ready

Edit Your Public Profile

Let me reiterate—my advice is to set your profile as public unless you have a very good reason for being anonymous or private.

Fill in as much detail as you can on your LinkedIn profile and remember to keep this updated as additional information becomes relevant. However, do be thoughtful about what you include, as all this information can be seen by your connections.

To illustrate: I am focused on building a big community to get more exposure for my blogs, so I am generous about whom I connect with. The problem with this approach is that when we share a lot of information, we make this information accessible to all new connections, which is probably how I end up on so many email marketing lists, the curse of the digital age! I am definitely more practiced at unsubscribing and blocking contacts than I used to be.

You can decide the information you want to be public. I didn't turn languages on, because I only speak one, but all other information is turned on. Unless you have a very good reason for more privacy. make everything public, or you'll never get all the benefits you can out of LinkedIn.

This is also why I don't share my phone number or address. Email, I can cope with. More phone calls or junk mail by post—not so much.

If your goal is to become an influencer, you must go beyond your immediate community to grow your reach and impact. Even if you don't want to *go big*, how often do you meet recruiters or potential employers online before you meet face-to-face? LinkedIn isn't Facebook, and you're here precisely because you want the right kind of exposure, *not* anonymity.

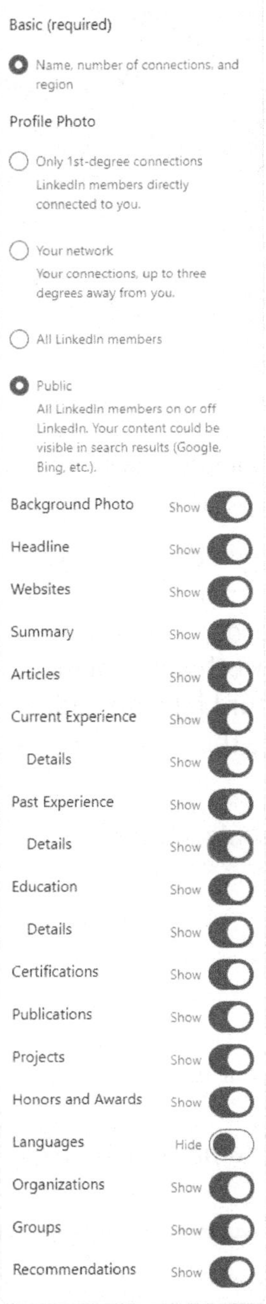

Figure 7. Setting what information is shared

Basic (required)

◉ Name, number of connections, and region

Profile Photo

○ Only 1st-degree connections
LinkedIn members directly connected to you.

○ Your network
Your connections, up to three degrees away from you.

○ All LinkedIn members

◉ Public
All LinkedIn members on or off LinkedIn. Your content could be visible in search results (Google, Bing, etc.).

Background Photo	Show ◉
Headline	Show ◉
Websites	Show ◉
Summary	Show ◉
Articles	Show ◉
Current Experience	Show ◉
Details	Show ◉
Past Experience	Show ◉
Details	Show ◉
Education	Show ◉
Details	Show ◉
Certifications	Show ◉
Publications	Show ◉
Projects	Show ◉
Honors and Awards	Show ◉
Languages	Hide ◉
Organizations	Show ◉
Groups	Show ◉
Recommendations	Show ◉

You can create a unique address for your LinkedIn profile, and this is a great opportunity to personalize your presence.

Why is this important? A personalized address makes it easier to promote and share your profile at events and on your email signature, your business cards, and your blog. When you share your Twitter handle or other social media assets, make sure you are maximizing your LinkedIn address as well. In fact, my professional names are the same across all my professional social media accounts.

Again, top right, click on *edit public profile & URL*.

Edit public profile & URL   ❷

Add profile in another language   ❷

Figure 8. Find where to edit your url

Then at the very top of the right-hand column, you'll see *edit your custom URL*.

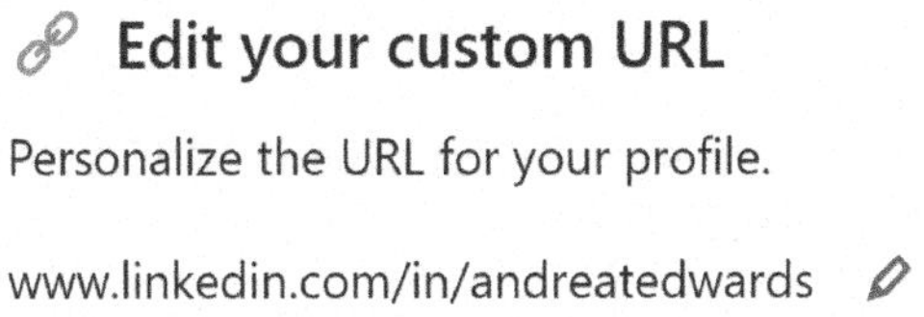

🔗 Edit your custom URL

Personalize the URL for your profile.

www.linkedin.com/in/andreatedwards ✏

Figure 9. Editing your url

This is a very simple process. Click on the pencil icon to get rid of the numbers and dashes in your name and put in the name you want.

Hint—Create a Consistent Professional Social Media Presence

If you have a consistent professional brand name across social media platforms, you'll be easier to find, and your promotion will be more effective. My handle, no matter the platform, is @AndreaTEdwards. If you are late doing this and someone else nabbed your name, you may need to be creative. Those with very common names often miss out on having their own names on their LinkedIn profile. If you have a Twitter profile already, I suggest using the same name. Either way, decide what is the right professional name for yourself on social media and then use it everywhere.

Once you've done this, remember to promote your social media name and link to your profiles in all the right places: as a permanent part of your email signature, in presentations, at the end of blogs, and on business cards.

A final point, the number of people who do not do this continues to surprise me. It's so easy to do, makes it easier to share your LinkedIn address, and you can use it in multiple ways. Get it done.

❑ **I've updated my LinkedIn web address to be my name (or close to it)**

This is What You Look Like Without a Photo

Figure 10. Faceless without a photo

Not having a photo on social media really is unacceptable. If you have no photo and try to connect with anyone who takes social media seriously, your request will often be rejected immediately. A profile without a photo effectively sends the following messages with your request:

- You don't take social media seriously and aren't worth the time.

- You have absolutely no idea what you are doing and don't deserve to be taken seriously.

- You are a bot or spam account, and none of us want to connect with these if we can avoid it.

Adding a photo means it's 14 times more likely your profile will be found and visited, and you are 36 times more likely to receive a message from a contact.

Update Your Profile Picture

So, let's just make sure we update our profile pictures, yes? Your photo needs to be relatively professional. It shouldn't be a photo of you sitting in your mum's kitchen or at a party with your mates, and always go for a simple, uncluttered background. If you don't have a photo, get your camera out (or phone, it's good enough these days) and ask someone to take a picture of you in front of a wall. Aim for something plain, though color or texture can nicely compliment your headshot.

Make sure the light is nice as well, with late afternoon light the best. If you're not sure about the best lighting, point your phone at your face and do a circle. The best light will be obvious, as it will make your skin look nicer.

A gentle suggestion: ask your photographer to stand above you to avoid a double chin. #justsayin

Specifications for your Profile Photo

You can upload JPG, GIF, or PNG files. The file size is 8MB maximum.

Your photo should be square.

The ideal pixel size for your photo is 400 x 400 or 7680 (W) by 4320 (H) pixels.

If either width or height exceeds 20,000 pixels, your photo will not upload.

For the most current information on photo size or any other details on LinkedIn, the best resource is LinkedIn help.[12]

A Google search can also provide this to you.

Once you have taken your photo, some careful photo editing can make for a brighter, more flattering headshot— it's amazing how many years you can take off! However, go easy with the editing tools. If you edit your photo too much, not only will it be obvious, but people might not recognize you when they meet you face-to-face. I've met a few people who were virtually unrecognizable in real life.

It's important to crop the photo as close to your face as you can, and LinkedIn suggests using a headshot with your face taking up 60% of the frame. This ensures a good headshot, not a tiny head with a big, distracting background. This is more important than ever, given that most people will view your image on their phones.

A simple check: how does your profile look on your phone? Can you even see your face? Is it clear?

LinkedIn Cover Story Video—New!

These cover story videos can be a maximum of 30 seconds long and it lives on your LinkedIn profile, residing in the same area as your profile photo. It doesn't replace your profile picture; they just co-exist.

After uploading your cover video, an orange-colored circle appears on the edges of your profile image. When people search for you, they will see the photo. When someone views your profile, the video will automatically play silently in your profile image circle. You activate the sound by clicking on the video.

---

12 https:// www.linkedin.com/ help

People with great video talent are doing an excellent job here. If you want to do it, look around for the best examples and take some inspiration before recording yours.

It's only 30 seconds, but that can feel like an eternity. Be clear in what you want to communicate—looking for a job, showcasing your skills, outlining your career to date, inspiring your community to take action, and so on—then script it, practice it, and only then shoot it. It's important to get this tight and right.

The best format is vertical to ensure you're maximizing the space, and for tips on how to do a great job, search for experts in creating video for LinkedIn. They are numerous.

Select a Banner Picture

The other important image is your banner, or the rectangular space above your profile photo on LinkedIn. And no, you can't do a video here. A good banner can make your profile pop, and it's an important opportunity for visual storytelling.

Sixty-three percent of the world's population are visual learners, so taking advantage of visual opportunities is always important. What kind of visual story should your banner tell? People choose lots of things, from corporate branding or themselves speaking onstage to suggestive imagery like city skylines, golf courses, green spaces, and oceans. Another option I recommend is colors and textures.

I change my banner often—in fact, right now it features my current book, *Uncommon Courage*. I generally change it as regularly as I can, at least every few months.

Before I had books to feature on my banner, my most frequent default banners were always "red bling," because red is my favorite color, and the bling makes me happy. I've used red sparkly hearts and red "dragon skin."

Remember to change your banner every few months, because nothing should be stagnant in the digital world.

I've often used my own photography for banners, but I'm very happy to spend money on visual assets. At a bare minimum, you should search for free stock photography and look for a color, texture, or idea that aligns with your personal theme.

Shutterstock is my stock photo library of choice. A key benefit of Shutterstock is their editing tool, which lets you upload images and customize them to the right size for all social media channels—all in one place. You can also add information directly to your photos, including social media handles and website information. If you don't want to outsource or you don't have the budget, using the tools available on professional stock photo sites is a possibility.

Hot tip: before designing it yourself, look at your LinkedIn profile on your computer and your mobile phone. Take note of where your profile picture is and make sure your design elements are not lost behind your profile picture.

Please remember that the most important money you will spend, if you take social media seriously, is on your imagery. It's critical if you want to gain traction and attention. The tools available online make it very easy for all of us to look professional on LinkedIn. In addition to the editing tools I mentioned above, the app Canva, among others, provides an array of free graphic design tools.

If you have a social media budget, I recommend going to sites like Fiverr.com and Upwork.com, where you can find a very affordable designer to create a personal banner that you can use on LinkedIn and any other sites or platforms you use for professional communication. Recent changes to the LinkedIn layout give you more space to work with than ever before, so definitely invest what you can and maximize this visual digital real estate!

LinkedIn Banner Specifications

The dimensions for the banner are minimum of 1584 (w) x 396 (h) pixels.

The file needs to be JPG, PNG, or GIF (maximum 8MB).

Here are six CEOs with consistently professional-looking profiles. Search their names to check out their current look on LinkedIn—including photo and banner:

Sir Richard Branson

Indra Nooyi

Jeff Weiner, CEO of LinkedIn

Arianna Huffington

Bill Gates

Ginni Rometty

Satya Nadella

The bottom line is that anyone who is active and serious on LinkedIn views a profile without a banner as an incomplete job. It tells us that this user does not understand the power of LinkedIn—they're just going through the motions. It's a small but important detail in having a complete profile. It's also a piece of digital real estate many people fail to maximize. Appeal to the visual learners amongst us—and look great too.

❏ **I've updated my photo**: make it a nice photo, it's representing you.

❏ **I've scripted, practiced and uploaded my mini-video on my profile**: do a great job here. It will help you stand out.

❏ **I've updated my banner**: do something that is meaningful to you, that visually shows who you are as a professional.

4 WRITE YOUR PROFESSIONAL HEADLINE

This might seem like a very small detail, but you should plan to spend a decent amount of time on this, as this is more important than meets the eye.

Your current role automatically populates this space, so as long as you have indicated a current role there will be information here already. The first three things people see on LinkedIn are your photo, your name, and your professional headline.

Figure 11. Your headline with photo and banner

Your headline is the text that follows your name. In the example above, the headline is *Inspiring leaders to own their voice with integrity and #UncommonCourage – a committed voice for a better future for all life on earth.*

Think of your headline as the place where you make your first impression.

When do Your Connections See Your Headline?

When they search for your name they see it, as it's now part of the search text, but not if you include additional information next to your name, which I'll talk about later

When you write a comment, they see it.

When you send an invitation, they see it.

When you participate in groups, they see it.

When they click on your profile, they see it.

When they read a blog you post, they see it.

It's Critical. So, What Should It Say?

I always recommend having a look at the kinds of headlines other people in your field are using. That being said, don't be afraid to be different—or a first in your industry. I often encourage very senior executives to use their job title, since they are senior enough that it's appropriate. However, there are many more ways to approach writing a headline.

Here are examples of some headlines from my contacts on LinkedIn—no preference or order.

Joanne FLINN—Sustainability: Economics + Environment, Social and Governance (ESG) for business results

Pravin Shekar—Outlier Marketer: Unconventional methods to grow your business!

Lindley Craig—Building better individuals who build better companies

Niklas Myhr, PhD—The Social Media Professor at Chapman University

Stacey Albert—Powering the curious to shape what's next!

Drew Calin—Helping companies hire the best talent, wherever they are.

Wendy (Hogan) McEwan—Chief of Staff, APJ

Lindsay Adams OAM—Add another stream of income to your business using Profiling Tools | DISC | Motivators | Performance Gap Indicator | Author | Australian Hall of Fame Speaker

Natasha David—Helping B2B champions find their voices and tell their stories

Dr Frank Hagenow, CSP—Global Speaker and CEO Coach supporting executives to build trustful relationships with employees and customers.

Tiffani Bova—Growth Advisor | Sales Strategist | Keynote Speaker | WSJ Bestselling Author | Thinkers50 | What's Next Podcast Host

Avi Z Liran—Global *Delightful Experience* and Organisational Culture Consultant, **TEDx** & CSP Keynote Speaker, Author, Trainer, Coach, and Mentor. Developing Delightful Leaders, Organizations, and Communities.

Gina Romero—Unconventional Entrepreneur. Community Builder. Inclusive Innovation, Women's Economic Empowerment, Digital Economy, AI and the Future of Work

Gabe Rijpma—Making Health Better – CEO at Aceso Health

Kerrie Phipps—Speaker, Leadership Coach, Author of "DO Talk To Strangers – How To Connect With Anyone, Anywhere" and Podcast

Andrew Psarianos—CEO weARVR.one and Picture Perfect Productions| Using Virtual Reality to improve Safety Training | L & D | Empathy. Storytelling and video content production. A global network of camera crews for remote shoots.

Stephanie Dickson—Founder Green Is The New Black • Host Live Wide Awake Podcast • Speaker

What Should Your Headline Be?

Which of these examples stood out to you? Perhaps you didn't like any of them. Would you prefer to feature your job title instead? There is no right answer, and I shared this collection to give you an idea of the variety of headlines professionals use for their LinkedIn profiles.

Note that only the first 50 characters of your headline are generally visible unless people are looking at your profile.

One approach when defining your title is to answer the question: ***whom do you help?*** Audience focus is everything, but if you take a look, most LinkedIn Headlines are not audience-focused at all.

So, can you fill in the dots?

"I help professionals..."

"I help businesses..."

Try using the following words to inspire new creative thinking: *I enable, empower, facilitate, inspire, encourage, galvanize, rouse, energize, support, unlock, build,* and so on. **An excellent thesaurus is a gift during this process.**

The important lesson is that in today's digital world, all content you create (including your social media profiles) should be focused on your audience, and this is your foremost opportunity to talk to *your* audience and tell them how *you* can help them.

As you may have noticed, many of the examples I provided above are from fairly creative fields or roles. That's because my community is a predominantly creative one, but that might not suit you. If none of these examples speaks to you, I recommend you look through *your* connections' professional headlines and take inspiration there.

Another very important strategy is to focus on **keywords relevant to your job because** LinkedIn is a search engine, and Google loves LinkedIn. What are the keywords for your industry?

Sales: sales, sales leadership, CRM, social selling expert

Marketing: customer experience, big data, content marketing, social media, growth hacker

Leadership: management, innovation, transformational leader, building talent, future of work

You may have noticed some professionals using the vertical line symbol— | —rather than commas between words or phrases in their LinkedIn title. Stars also make an appearance on LinkedIn today, as do ticks, dots, and other images, but is it your style? It's not mine, which is why I don't use images or symbols in my headline—apart from what is now my primary hashtag #UncommonCourage. Do what feels right for you. These visual elements certainly help if you want to stand out a little more.

If you are a senior business leader, the common practice is to use your title. The higher up you are, the more sense this makes. However, consider using your title *and* making it personal by writing a mini-statement at the end to embody who you are.

Two examples

—*making a difference...*

—*a transformational leader with a passion*

Adding a brand to your name

When I published the first edition of this book, I had **Andrea T Edwards, CSP—The Digital Conversationalist** as my name. When I established my company, I decided that my name and brand needed to be synonymous, which is why **The Digital Conversationalist** was included with my name on my profile. You can do this too.

However, since then, LinkedIn changed the rules, and one of the changes is it punishes users who do this. You will not appear regularly to your audiences when you add a title to your name. Think of it as an algorithm punishment. So perhaps it might be worth removing this if you still do it?

- Keeping on top of the changing rules is important and I recommend looking at these two pages to avoid ending up in LinkedIn jail: LinkedIn's professional community policies[13]

- LinkedIn's user agreement[14]

When you are an employee, it's always important to ask yourself what's appropriate. Only you can answer this question because your job, your industry, and the culture of

---

13 https://www.linkedin.com/legal/professional-community-policies
14 https://www.linkedin.com/legal/user-agreement

your business need to be considered. Whatever you do, please don't be afraid to have your own style, while understanding the rules and limitations that might be in play. On the other hand, never do something you're not comfortable with or feel pressured to follow the crowd.

Back to Your Professional Headline

In this section, you have 120 characters to use (including spaces). If you don't write a professional headline in your own style, your current job title will automatically be used. That is fine, but why not use the space to make an impact and let your audience know you better?

I encourage you to be bold if it feels right. Stand out. Be brave. And be you.

Draft your headline. Try several, it may take some exploration to develop. If you have marketing friends, ask them to help you.

_____

_____

_____

_____

❑ My headline reflects me, so be appropriate, be bold, and be authentically myself.

Four Additions to Your Primary Profile — NEW

Figure 12. The four new elements in your profile

1. Record your name

Figure 13. The speaker

This little speaker image provides the opportunity to record your name in your voice. Do it. Even if you think your name is easy to pronounce or understand, on a global platform, with multiple pronunciations of every name, this is a great little add-on. Click on the pencil in the top right of your profile to get to this section.

2. Pronouns

You can also add pronouns, which is more and more common today. There are four options.

- She/her
- He/him
- They/them
- Custom

I only added pronouns recently, before that, I figured I'd been around long enough for it to be pretty obvious. But since so many others believe pronouns are important to their identity and how they want to be seen, I decided to add it out of respect and solidarity. It's up to you, but this is one of those small societal changes that harms no one and honors others for how they want to be referred to.

Click on the pencil in the top right of your profile to get to this section.

3. Talks about (aka creator mode)

Below your professional summary is an opportunity to feature hashtags on what you talk about.

Talks about #courage, #climatecrisis, #employeeadvocacy, #knowledgeeconomy, and #socialleadership

Figure 14. Personal hashtags in your profile

To get to this, scroll down on your LinkedIn profile page to *Your Dashboard*. Click on *creator mode* at the top of the list of three. Turn it on and then add five hashtags relevant to you. Creator mode is important for anyone committed to building their profile by actively engaging and sharing content on LinkedIn.

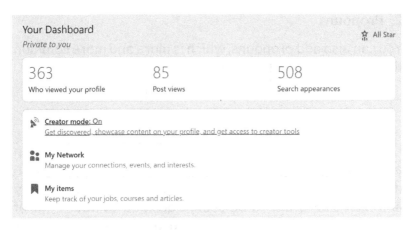

Figure 15. Setting creator mode

Don't know which hashtags to use? There's more on hashtags later in this book, but another option is to look at profiles similar to yours. Be inspired by what they are using. Remember, if you use popular hashtags on LinkedIn, they will gain more traction.

How do you know what's a popular hashtag? When you look at LinkedIn (not your profile) in the left column, there is a list of hashtags you already follow. LinkedIn may have selected some for you, based on past engagement. If none are there, go to the next step.

Followed Hashtags

\# womeninleadership

\# ceo

\# climatechange

\# greenenergy

\# climatefinance

\# biodiversity

\# climateemergency

\# sustainabledevelopment

Figure 16.
Followed hashtags list

\# climatecrisis

\# linkedin

At the bottom of this list of hashtags is **_Discover More_**. Click on this and again, look down the left-hand column and you will see **_#Hashtags_** at the bottom of the list. Click on **_#Hashtags_** and you will see the ones you follow, suggestions of what to follow, and most importantly, how many people are already following these hashtags.

An example:

Figure 17. Hashtags have follower lists

Low follower numbers don't mean low value, but if you have a combination of high follower numbers and high-value hashtags (based on your priorities), you will attract the right audience.

A final note on creator tools. The two creator tools I currently have available are below, and it's worth exploring this section as it will continue to evolve. If you are a creator, it's important to understand this feature and what's possible. If you're wondering whether you have access to LinkedIn Live, this is where you can find it.

Creator tools

Creator mode gives you new ways to reach your audience by enabling access to the available tools. Learn more about creator tool access.

LinkedIn Live   ✔ Available ❯

Newsletters   ✔ Available ❯

Figure 18. Creator tools

4. Providing services, open to work, and hiring

On all our profiles, we now have a section at the bottom, with the title providing services (scroll across if you can't see this) with *Open to Work* and *Hiring* usually in the primary position.

Adding services is a simple update to make. Select the key services you offer (it's all pre-populated), add some media (only images allowed, at the time of writing) and you're good to go.

It is not yet possible to integrate existing testimonials or recommended skills on LinkedIn. In the meantime, request reviews, and make sure you rate your connections, so they can build their profile in this section too. Give to get.

> Providing services ✎
> Corporate Training, Executive Coaching, Leadership Development, Public Speaking, Training, Marketing Consu...
> See all details

Figure 19. Services you provide

There are two other sections—*open to work* and *hiring*. You may have seen people open to being hired because a green "open for work" banner appears on their profile picture. If you do not want this to be public, you can keep it private.

As an example, consider my friend Avi Liran's profile. He has both *Providing services* and a *Hiring* section. His profile picture is updated with a purple #Hiring banner, which increases the chances of a potential candidate finding this opportunity.

Figure 20. Your profile shows purple when you are hiring

Avi Z Liran · 1st

| Providing services
Management Consulting, HR Consulting, Customer ...
See all details | Hiring a Sales Development Representative
Delivering Delight · Philippines (Remote) · 6 days ago
See all details |

Figure 21. What you are looking for when you're hiring

Make sure you update your profile and use all the different elements available to you to ensure an all-star profile.

Actions:

❑ I've reviewed and updated my core profile so it's current

❑ My name is voice recorded so others can say it correctly

If I intend to grow my reach, impact, and connections, I have also:

❑ Turned on creator mode

❑ Added relevant #Hashtags

❑ Considered and even turned on creator Tools

If I am hiring or looking for work, I have:

❑ Turned on and filled in these profile elements!

5 TIME TO
WRITE YOUR SUMMARY

Now it's time to focus on your professional summary, and this is really important. A little exploration of profiles from your industry will show you that there are many different approaches to writing this section. There is no right or wrong way; what matters is to tell your story and feel good about it. In this section, I'll outline what I believe makes an effective summary.

Write it in the first person. That may feel uncomfortable for you, as it does for many people, but it comes across as more genuine in the first person. To overcome any qualms, write it in the third person, and once you're happy with it, flip it into the first person. This will give you permission to be bold.

What to write? It's a snapshot of your professional career, what you do, and what you focus on. Remember to include keywords relevant to your industry. LinkedIn will encourage you to do this, but as an example, if you are in sales, include terms such as sales, sales leadership, or customer service. This is how you will be found when professionals are searching LinkedIn for people like you.

But don't just write about your work. Write about your values, what you care about, what you stand for—and please, don't be afraid to use humor especially if you are naturally a funny person. This is about you, the person because you're not a machine. It's important to write this section in a way that will engage readers. There are enough boring summaries out there—why stay in that herd?

Also, resist the temptation to make this section read like a resume or CV. That information should be available in your position descriptions throughout the rest of your LinkedIn profile, so try not to double up on what you have already said. Tell people a story. Let them get to know you and the type of person you are. Do you care about women's issues? Talk about it here. Is employee engagement close to your heart? Tell us why and how. Are you passionate about technology and its potential to change the world? Great—share that passion. Is the environment your hot issue? Put it in your summary.

I also advise that you do not use bullet points to highlight your achievements in your summary. Visually, bullets don't look good on LinkedIn anyway, as the platform isn't designed for them. Furthermore, there is plenty of real estate on LinkedIn to list your achievements—in your position descriptions and awards sections, for example. Use your summary to get people excited about who you are and your passions.

Adding Visuals to your Profile – NEW!

One significant recent change is that the visual elements moved from the *Summary* section to a new *Featured* section.

This is good as the *Featured* section is bolder, bigger, and more front and center in your profile.

However, what it does mean is that your last article now only appears as a normal post. This means you need to pick what you want to feature to include your original content.

This is how the *Featured* section looks now—much bigger and bolder.

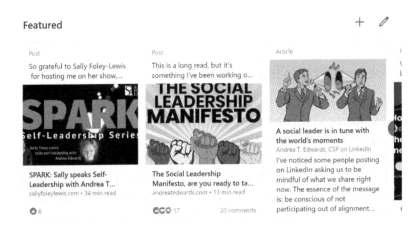

Figure 22. Bolder features

Below is the *Activities* section, which shows your latest activity on LinkedIn. If it's empty, you are not doing anything on LinkedIn at all.

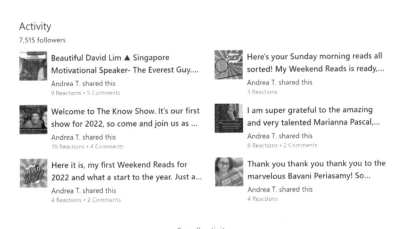

Figure 23. More visibility for your activities

To get to your articles, click on *see all activity* at the bottom of the section, and across the top, select *articles* to see your articles or blogs published directly to LinkedIn.

Andrea T.'s Activity

(All activity) (Articles) (Posts) (Documents)

Figure 24. Accessing activities, articles, posts, and documents

This means your audience must take another step to get to your articles. And people don't always like to take an extra step, do they? This along with the increase in characters for a regular LinkedIn post, has reduced the number of articles people are publishing.

It's still valuable for you to post articles.

When you publish long-form content as a post in the stream instead of using an article, you'll see your posts get lost in the history of LinkedIn. Posting an article means it will always have a place. This means it's easier to find this content and every other article you've published. Given this element of stability, I still prefer posting articles for long-form content.

Use the *Featured* Section

To ensure your latest content is featured, I encourage you to take this step. Every time you publish an article, click the + button on *Featured* to add your latest LinkedIn article to that section. You can remove it when you publish your next one, ensuring your latest article is front and center on your profile.

Figure 25. Find this with the + button above the Featured section

Above is the window that opens. Simply click on the + button for the option to add posts, articles, links, or media. This feature is a recent addition, and it's a great opportunity to highlight anything timely or significant you've contributed on LinkedIn. To remove posts before adding new ones, simply click on the pencil and then *remove from featured.*

Another recent addition you may see in the list above, if LinkedIn has already rolled it out for your part of the world, is **Newsletters**. By adding this to your featured section, you will attract new audiences and up your subscriber numbers. Check it out when it becomes available to you.

But I don't have a *Featured* Section on My LinkedIn profile!

Many users miss out on the visual elements available on their LinkedIn profile, simply by not realizing what's possible. Please prioritize this. If people are interested in you and what you have to say, you want to be able to give them the opportunity to dig deeper into you and your work.

To develop this aspect of your profile, look below the *About* section for the *Featured* section. Then click the *Add Featured* hyperlink. Now add a selection of posts, articles, links, or media.

Some Ideas on What to Add to *Features* if You're Drawing a Blank:

- Photos (media)—at work, with your team, on company outings, onstage, with influential people

- A recent post you're particularly proud of

- Links to media coverage, podcast interviews, YouTube videos

- Previous blog posts or articles—you might be posting your articles on LinkedIn or Medium, as well as on your own website or a company website. When you feature your content here, you can lead your audience to your other important digital assets, especially ones you own.

- Your website, if you want to drive people there

- Links to SlideShare to show off your latest presentation

- A PDF of something compelling that you want to share (LinkedIn likes documents, too!)

There's so much you can do. You can do it for your professional roles too, in your experience section below.

This is a wonderful opportunity to tell your audience the story of your career, visually. Visual storytelling is easy to do, offers visual learners a more compelling learning opportunity, and rounds out your profile to be more engaging on multiple levels. Maximize this opportunity.

Pro tip: if you don't already do so, make it a point to capture your professional moments from this day forward.

Remember, as with all aspects of your LinkedIn profile, keep updating your *Featured* section with new content and fresh images.

Finding great LinkedIn profiles is easier these days; just scroll through your contacts to find good ones. Note: as you do this, you'll see many unfinished profiles. They don't look as polished as the good ones.

Over the years, I'm always researching to find the best people with the most compelling summaries on the platform.

LinkedIn's most searched profiles or Power Profiles are a useful reference point. While people may be *looking* for them, not all of them are embracing all the powerful features that LinkedIn offers—as evidenced by their incomplete profiles.

I see so many missed opportunities on LinkedIn, and often it comes down to the basic stuff, such as not writing a compelling summary, not telling a visual story, or having a poor-quality profile photo. The good news is that if you complete your profile engagingly and intelligently, you'll automatically have a better LinkedIn profile than most people out there!

There are many great examples where you can find inspiration. But your job, once you've learned all you can from other people's profiles, is to decide on a style that suits you.

If you want to take some inspiration from professionals that are being celebrated on LinkedIn, google LinkedIn Top Voices or Power List of the Top Voices.

What Makes a Poor Summary?

Summaries written in the third person. I strongly suggest using the first person if you want to tell a genuine story and reach people's hearts and minds.

Writing summaries as a career overview. We can look through your LinkedIn profile for that—tell us something we don't know.

Failing to tell a visual story—don't miss this important opportunity, but it's in the *Featured* section now.

Failing to tell a story that helps the world understand what sort of a person you are. We are bringing the whole person to work today, so be authentic and real in your summary.

Support for Writing Your Summary

The following fill-in-the-blank sentences will help you create a great and meaningful summary:

I have been in...

Throughout my career, I have valued/focused on...

I care about...

...is important to me.

I have lived and worked in...

...has taught me...

Make writing an effective summary a priority. It's natural to feel daunted by this because we are not all born storytellers and writing about ourselves can feel uncomfortable. Ask for help if you need it but do the work yourself. Tell your own story. If you completely outsource this piece, I guarantee it won't come across as authentic.

If you can make it a priority to write your summary, it will help you be successful in completing and being proud of your profile. **Don't get stuck here,** as people often do. Just get it done. On the other hand, if you just can't do it, don't let it hold you back from participating on LinkedIn. Move on until you feel comfortable writing an engaging summary about yourself.

If you're really stuck, find a LinkedIn buddy at the same stage as you, and do it together step-by-step, helping each other with these elements. Perhaps that is the trick to give you the confidence you need?

And remember, write and save it as a file on your computer. Don't write straight into the summary section, because sometimes it doesn't upload, and you lose all that work! Set up a LinkedIn folder and put everything in one place for future reference.

Notes—list my keywords, statements, and points I want to make as a leader in my field.

_____

_____

_____

_____

❑ **I've updated my summary:** It's in first person and I'm happy to have it read. It shows me as a full well-rounded career person.

6 COVER YOUR HISTORY, UPDATE YOUR POSITIONS

The older you are, the longer this is going to take, but it's critical to make sure your entire career history is up to date. If you have an old resume, print it out as a reference to use while you fill in your LinkedIn profile.

Keep in mind that even in this section, you can give yourself permission to not be boring. The further back you go, the less you will feel inclined to add information, but include as much as you can, even if it is just the job title, company, and employment dates. Talk about achievements, what you loved about the job, and maybe even why you moved on—if it's positive and relevant. You can tell a wonderful story across your career span.

If you have career gaps, don't be afraid to explain them, for gaps are becoming more and more accepted in the business world today, especially for the younger generation, who are changing roles faster than ever before. Long-term travel, parenting, sabbaticals, time off for education, and other reasons for career breaks are not things to hide. Trust in the human truth that the right employers will value your life experience.

Once you have entered all your text content, the next step is reviewing the way you use visual elements. I recommend adding photos, links, SlideShare decks, or YouTube videos for every role that you list. If you don't have relevant images for past roles, add some inspirational messages.

Try and use images that mean something to you or show you participating in something, and also remember to include images of the company you worked with. The images don't necessarily have to be of you—but keep in mind that this is about celebrating your career, so don't be shy. And please, don't let these images be static. Keep updating them and shuffling the order, especially in your current position and summary.

Here's what you currently see under my top three current positions, and I update this regularly!

Figure 26. Your images add to the story your summary tells

This goes all the way back to my first job as a musician in the Australian Army.

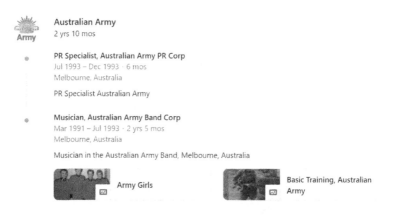

Figure 27. Even your very first job

I'm telling a story here. People are curious to meet the gal who served in the military early in her career, and as a professional musician to boot!

What's unique, intriguing, and worth sharing as part of your story?

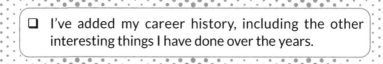

❑ I've added my career history, including the other interesting things I have done over the years.

7 FOLLOW
COMPANIES, THE MEDIA, AND INFLUENCERS

Recruitment remains a core part of LinkedIn, but its primary focus is as a content platform, and as such, it's only as powerful an influence as *you* set it up to be. I've said it before: when you get to the point where you are checking LinkedIn on the weekend the way you would Instagram, TikTok, or Facebook, you'll know you've upped your LinkedIn game to make it a rich and valuable platform for yourself, personally and professionally.

The best way to bring LinkedIn's phenomenal power as a content platform into your life and news feed is by following great people and businesses. You can follow influencers, companies, news sources, hashtags (more in the next section), and, of course, the best people you know. Doing so will make your LinkedIn news feed a rich information platform, which means you'll visit and engage with it every day.

When people complain that their LinkedIn feed is full of nonsense, I say to them, it's only as good as who and what you follow. If it's full of nonsense, unfollow those who do not inspire you and focus on following the best there is.

Start with Influencers

I'm going to talk later about the increasing importance of hashtags, but as a starting point, LinkedIn influencers are worth following.

There are over 500 official **LinkedIn influencers**, including high-level business leaders, public figures (such as presidents and prime ministers), authors, celebrities, and speakers.[15] In today's world, anyone can become an influencer on any platform, but the exclusivity of LinkedIn influencers makes it an audience that stands out.

Following your favorite LinkedIn influencers is also a great way to fill your news feed with awesome content—and it's shareable content too. Bill Gates and Sir Richard Branson are two of my favorites, and there are many you can follow, across so many fields and specialties.

Who are LinkedIn Influencers?

You can tell someone is an official LinkedIn influencer when they have the small blue LinkedIn logo next to their name. Some examples:

Narendra Modi [in]
Prime Minister of India

Oprah Winfrey [in]
CEO, Producer, Publisher, Actress and Innovator

Ian Bremmer [in]
President at Eurasia Group

Gary Vaynerchuk [in]
Chairman of VaynerX, CEO of VaynerMedia, 5-Time NYT...

---

15 For more information on LinkedIn influencers, read this article. https://www.linkedin.com/help/linkedin/answer/a516942/linkedin-influencers

Deepak Chopra MD (official)
Founder at Deepak Chopra LLC

Arianna Huffington
Founder and CEO at Thrive Global

Jeff Haden
Speaker, Inc. Magazine contributing editor, author of...

Christine Lagarde
President of the European Central Bank

Simon Sinek
Optimist and Author at Simon Sinek Inc.

Sallie Krawcheck
CEO and Co-Founder of Ellevest

Figure 28. LinkedIn influencers

Influencers will appear as suggestions in the right-hand column of your LinkedIn profile, or if not there, go to your profile, down to the bottom of the left-hand column, and click on **Discover More**, just below the followed hashtags column.

Followed Hashtags

\# womeninleadership

\# ceo

\# climatechange

Show more ⌄

Discover more

Figure 29.
Use followed hashtags

If you want to make it easier, search LinkedIn for high-profile people you respect and admire, then follow them. If they've got the blue LinkedIn logo, you'll know they are an official influencer.

Looking for More Inspiration on Whom to Follow?

Beyond the official 500+ influencers, search for and follow professionals who are influential in your field, the top influencers on LinkedIn in your country, and the top influencers in fields you are passionate about.

Do a quick Google search to find influencer lists like Top 30 To Follow or simply Biggest Voices in [the field of your choice].

Companies

You should also follow companies: the company you work for (if applicable), companies you admire, and companies that are delivering world-class business information relevant to you. McKinsey, for example, remains a favorite business information source. If you have strategic customers or partners, you should follow them too. And what about companies that just fascinate you? For example, I follow Disney because it's a business built on storytelling, and I am intrigued with how it speaks to the world. What companies intrigue you or strike your fancy?

If you're on the job hunt, following the companies you want to work for should be a no-brainer, as well as reviewing their LinkedIn company page/s before an interview. With that said, many companies are still not doing a great job with content on their company pages because they still see

LinkedIn as nothing more than a recruitment platform. The content landscape is improving as corporates slowly realize LinkedIn is about delivering empowering information that helps customers, not just talking about how great your business is, but it's been a slow journey of change.

I recommend checking out your own company page (follow it while you're there!) to see how it strikes you. Is it compelling enough to entice you to learn from it every day? Is it good enough to attract customers or prospects? That should be any company's minimum goal. If it's full of business achievements and awards your company has won, it is not delivering anything meaningful to customers and it won't draw people in every day.

Company pages are only valuable when they bring actual value to their audience—and that is not just employees or prospective employees. You can be proud of the awards your company achieved, but if that is all your business showcases, it's about you, not about the audience you want to attract.

If you have any role in creating or maintaining your organization's LinkedIn company page, remember it is a place to deliver value to your audience. It's not a soapbox for your business, which is how too many companies continue to use it.

So, start following companies that are meaningful to you and you'll get the content they create in your LinkedIn feed. Search what they're sharing before following through. If they're not doing a great job on LinkedIn, following them could just put more dross in your timeline.

News sources

News and media used to be in a different section on LinkedIn, including specific topics to follow, but now topics have moved under hashtags—which makes sense! Regardless, most global news channels are available on LinkedIn, so following them is a great way to keep up to date with news and views relevant to your field and expertise. Whatever your news habits, following the most compelling sites will ensure that your LinkedIn feed is rich with information that is relevant and helpful to you.

Click on **Discover More** in the left-hand column of your LinkedIn feed, scroll down, and hopefully, you'll see media companies coming up as suggestions. If you can't find your favorites, search for them in the search bar and follow.

LinkedIn's search bar is always at the top on the left of any LinkedIn page.

Figure 30. The search function

Hot tip #1 with the new layout.

It has never been easier to follow interesting people and entities. Scroll down your profile and if you've already set up your *Interests*, you can scroll across influencers, companies, groups, and schools.

Figure 31. Use your interests to find people to follow

Hot tip #2 for connections

Go to your favorite connections' profiles, and in the top right, you'll see a little bell next to the LinkedIn logo.

Figure 32. Get notified with the bell

1. When it's white, you'll get notifications of top posts from your favorite connection.

2. When it's black, you'll get notifications of all posts from your favorite connections.

This is another great way to manage what you see on LinkedIn.

I've followed:

(Tick off when completed)

❑ My company on LinkedIn

❑ Companies I admire, companies I want to work for, businesses I work with today

❑ A selection of the top 500+ LinkedIn influencers / peers I admire, my friends and former colleagues

❑ The media I track

8 USE HASHTAGS

Hashtags, once the cryptic language of Twitter, are hugely relevant today across Facebook, Twitter, Pinterest, Instagram, YouTube, Snapchat, TikTok and, since August 2016, LinkedIn.[16] Still, many people do not use them.

Introducing hashtags and subsequently increasing their importance on the platform has made LinkedIn an even more powerful social force in the corporate world. Hashtags link you to everyone else using a particular hashtag, allowing you to join a global conversation on your topic of expertise. It's how you get and keep attention and how you elevate your brand and voice to be heard beyond your immediate community (aka your first-degree connections).

Unless you use hashtags, you are basically invisible to anyone who is not directly connected to you. Far from being teen slang or for significant events only, hashtags are a critical factor in building a bigger profile and a strong personal brand.

Hashtags link you to the people and ideas you care about most—and to the people searching for information on the topics you speak out on. It's how you build your profile beyond

---

16 https://blog.linkedin.com/2016/08/25/tap-into-professional-knowledge-with¬
content-search-at-linkedin

your immediate network. It's how you get aligned to and establish yourself as an expert on the topics you care about, digitally. If you want to be a powerhouse on social media, hashtags are essential.

Hashtags are relevant to global and topical conversations (or #moments), but they are also relevant to industries, job titles, and core topics of expertise.

A few examples across some core topics:

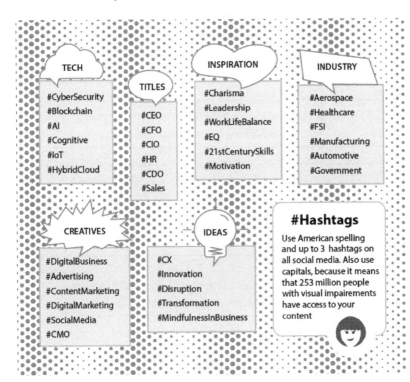

Figure 33. Hashtag have topics

To become known as an expert in your field, use hashtags relevant to the core topics in your field, especially if you want to grow your profile beyond your immediate community. Don't know what are the right hashtags to use? Look at the ones your peers are using.

Here's some hashtags that have appeared on my feed from my connections. You can tell the topics from the main ones, and then there is a selection of hashtags that are unique to you or your business. That's absolutely the right combination, although advise only using three hashtags at a time on LinkedIn. The LinkedIn algorithm prioritizes the first three hashtags, so limit yourself and choose them well. Use them at the end of your post, rather than embedding them the way a lot of people do. Hashtagging words within sentences makes your posts hard to read.

#boardgovernance #sustainablefuture #greensight

#startup #healthcare #stemcells #reprogramming #tech #people #biotechnology #research

#growth #whatinspiresme #education #personaldevelopment

#oilgas #financeandeconomy #banks #banking #gas

#thelionacademy, #empoweringpeople, #dionjensen, #2022chooseyou, #lisawestgate, #themisfithub

#costreduction #procurement #accountancy #business #icaew

Figure 34. Good hashtagging

Here are Some of the Hashtags I Follow

Following and using these hashtags not only attracts people to me, it also helps me find people interested in the same topics or issues as me. Furthermore, people who are third-degree connections sometimes appear in my feed because they are using a hashtag I am interested in. This provides an opportunity to build more connections who care about the same issues, and I can follow them or become connected to them. Building a network of people passionate about the same issues is one of the beauties of LinkedIn and all social media.

Figure 35. List of hashtags on LinkedIn

To follow hashtags on LinkedIn, simply click on **Discover More**. A list of options will appear (also in the left column), and hashtags will appear there. See all the hashtags you can follow? Go through this vast list and follow the ones that are most meaningful to you. Don't forget to pay attention to the number of followers, too. That said, lower numbers on the right hashtag for you are important to follow too. Big numbers aren't everything when it comes to social media, even if all the messaging is saying so. It may help you to find more targeted, niche, content that it's relevant to you.

And it *really is* how you bring LinkedIn—as a content and connections platform—to life. If you use hashtags well, you can easily open your profile up to third-degree connections, who will see you featured in their news feeds based on your hashtag use.

This brilliant evolution toward hashtags will tackle so many of the challenges LinkedIn continues to face, from a noisy nonsense-content perspective. But it means we must all get into the habit of using hashtags and using them intelligently—everywhere, but especially on LinkedIn.

Which Hashtags Should You Follow?

What hashtags are the thought leaders in your field using? LinkedIn might not be the best place to discover this, since so many people are still not using them, so check other social platforms too.

If you work for a company, what are the common company hashtags you could be using to tie yourself into a bigger global conversation? Check your company's social media profiles if you don't know what those hashtags are. It's usually pretty straightforward—#Microsoft #IBM #JPMorgan #DHL.

Twitter and Instagram are great sites to search for hashtags, and so is Facebook these days, even if you don't have an account. Twitter is great for keeping an eye on trending hashtags, while Instagram and Facebook show you how popular a hashtag is by tracking the number of times it has been used. In 2020 the number one hashtag in the world was #PhotoOfTheDay. Now it's in third place, and #Love is number one.[17] That's nice, isn't it?

Use the sites hashtags.org, top-hashtags.com, and hashtagify.com as reference points in your research.

Let's look at some topics and the hashtags linked to each. This is just a sampling.

Artificial intelligence: #AI #ArtificialIntelligence #animation #GameDev #IndieDev #3dart #3dModeling #MachineLearning #TechTwitter #infotech #architecture #Bots #DigitalTransformation #CyberSecurity #Blockchain #DX #Analytics #Industry40 #IIoT #IoT #aiArt #art #brutalism #AugmentedReality #web3

Engineering: #engineering #Hydraulics #IT #Telecom #Engineering #AWS #Data #ML #aviation #aviationlovers #3DPrinting #AI #ArtificialIntelligence #Healthcare #HealthTech #Futureofwork #innovation #PPDC #Engineering #solarpanels #renewableenergy #energyeffieciency #cleanenergy

The Metaverse: #Metaverse #AltoCityNFT #NFTs #DeFi #tokens #NFTCommmunity #nft #cryptocurrency #P2E #nftart #MINTING #ETH #BSC #NFTGame #MetaOasisDAO #DAO #sandbox #VirtualLand #VirtualWorlds #VirtualReality #AugmentedReality #NFTs #NFT #NFTart #NFTCommunity #NFTcollector #ETH #NFTartists #digitalart #Decentraland #web3

---

17 https://influencermarketinghub.com/most-popular-instagram-hashtags/

The climate emergency: #ClimateCrisis #ClimateChange #ClimateEmergency #ClimateAction #ClimateStrike #ClimateCrisisIsReal #Sustainability #SustainableLiving #ConsciousLiving #LittleGreenSteps #ClimateCrisisKills #DefendTheDefenders #DontLookUp #Extinction #6thMassExtinction #greenhousegases #environmentalist #pollution #stopclimatechange #deforestation #environment #sustainability #nature #globalwarming #savetheplanet #climate

The best hashtag tip: go to Twitter, Instagram, or even the LinkedIn list of hashtags and do a search with a basic term relevant to your industry or profession. Start there and you'll build a list of relevant hashtags. If you're feeling old, speak to the teenagers and millennials in your life. 😊

Remember, no one owns hashtags, and the possibilities are endless. You don't need to use one that already exists—you can start a trend. However, using well-established hashtags is a good way to elevate your visibility in your field.

How Hashtags are being Used on LinkedIn: the Good, the Bad, and the Terrible

Using hashtags is a new practice for many active LinkedIn users. And if you've been using them elsewhere, don't make the mistake of using hashtags on LinkedIn the same way you do on other platforms. It's important to understand how to harness and tailor their power specifically for LinkedIn. You will find the practices I'll discuss are relevant across other platforms, too.

Example one: only hashtags

#truelove #humanity #love #life

Figure 36. Poor hashtagging

Using hashtags as the only text-based content in your post delivers no value to your audience, even if it gets you into a healthy spot in LinkedIn's back-end. Please, never miss an opportunity to bring something meaningful to your audience. Remember, it's about them, not you. Tell people *why* you're sharing information and finish with hashtags. Remember to focus on three hashtags. While platforms like Instagram welcome up to ten, limit it to three on LinkedIn. Honestly, you shouldn't need more than that.

Example two: hashtags embedded within the post

When you write with hashtags instead of words in the middle of sentences, it requires a lot of effort to read your post. You don't want to make anything hard to read or unclear on social media, so keep hashtags separate from the content and put them—sparingly—at the end of your post.

Watch to find out why 300 people signed up for this zoomside chat unravelling #web3, #metaverse, #nfts, #playtoearn, #blockchaingaming with Robby Yung GB HK, CEO of Animoca Brands. Guaranteed to learn many practical lessons!

Figure 37. Worse hashtagging #1

or

Olaf Scholz announced #germany will use #g7 presidency to "turn that group into the nucleus of an international climate club." This could have big implications for countries like #australia - #climateaction #climatechange #energypolicy #netzero #2030vision Harriet Kater Blair Palese Ketan Joshi Florian Popp

Figure 38. Worse hashtagging #2

Example three: perfect

The idea that firms must choose between 'purpose' and 'performance' is just flat-out wrong. But shareholders and business leaders (including boards) clearly need to better communicate the link, since it's only going to get stronger. #esg #sustainability #corporatevalues #corporatebranding

Figure 39. Great hashtagging

Do your research and understand what hashtags look like when they're done right. Concisely say what you want to say, add the relevant hashtags, copy the relevant people, and you'll have a winner—not only in my books but based on research across social media. Take note of what works in posts you like, but it's ultimately up to you to decide how you will approach using hashtags.

The ongoing evolution in hashtag use on LinkedIn puts the information you're interested in at the forefront of what the platform is all about, so:

- Work out what hashtags you should be using.

- Follow hashtags on topics that are important to you.

- Use hashtags to get your content in front of new and relevant audiences.

- Build a hashtag habit.

- Put them at the end of your comments, but don't overdo your use of hashtags.

And finally, try not to be overwhelmed by hashtags, if you haven't yet acquired the habit of effectively using them. Trust me, it doesn't take much effort to turn yourself into a hashtag champion.

Hashtags empower you to be present in global conversations and they allow people to find you. This means they can engage with you, follow you, or track you, which opens more opportunities for you to become a valuable leader to them and influence the conversations that define your field.

Some additional hashtag guidance:

- Use one hashtag consistently if you work for a company. If you work for IBM, use #IBM and two others.

- If you want to be a thought leader in a particular sector, use common hashtags for that sector, such as #FSI #Insurance #Biotech #Healthcare or #Aerospace.

- If you're in a specific role, like marketing, use the most relevant hashtags: #Marketing #CMO #DigitalMarketing #CX #BigData #Analytics #SocialMedia #Advertising or #Branding.

- If you're targeting a specific role, like a CIO, common useful hashtags include #CIO #ITDirector #Cloud #HybridCloud #BigData #AI #CognitiveComputing #Storage #IoT #Collaboration #Productivity and #FutureOfWork.

- If you're in a field like wellness or mindfulness, use hashtags such as #Wellness #WholenessAt Work #Mindfulness #NLP #MindfulnessInBusiness #Selfleadership and #Meditation.

❑ **I've identified 6–8 hashtags.** Between my company, my industry or area of thought leadership, my role, topics that are relevant and topics that interest you, here are my top 8 to get started with:

1. _____

2. _____

3. _____

4. _____

5. _____

6. _____

7. _____

8. _____

9 INCLUDE PEOPLE, BUSINESSES, AND PUBLICATIONS IN YOUR POSTS

Social media is all about engaging in conversations and growing your community. In addition to using hashtags to draw people and companies to you, you should also copy publications, businesses, and people when it's relevant to do so.

Tagging is when you use the @ symbol with a name or business name. This person or business is now included in your post and gets an alert that you shared information.

There are many positions to take on tagging. I don't mind being tagged in posts sometimes, but there is also a *lot* of nonsense going on. Social media etiquette is an unspoken agreement between us, and tagging people is one of its finest arts.

When you tag someone, you put the responsibility on the person tagged to interact with the post. Most people will feel a strong sense of obligation to respond. We're human, and that's a lovely trait of humanity. These interactions can be engaging and enriching both for participants and the larger community. But tagging—and the obligation it creates—should not be taken too far.

Here's an example. If you're sharing an article from *Fortune Magazine,* use @Fortune to find the publication's LinkedIn profile and copy it into your post. (If *Fortune* didn't have a LinkedIn page, it wouldn't come up as an option to tag.) Make sure you select the right entity from the drop-down list that appears—see the image below.

You can do the same on other social sites too, including Facebook and Twitter.

Using @ to tag a person or organization is called "at-mentioning."

Figure 40. Use @ to find people and organizations

Expecting a response from *Fortune Magazine* may be setting your expectations too high. If you're famous or infamous, maybe you will get a reply. But it doesn't happen a lot, so don't count on it. However, you are giving credit where credit is due, and this is correct social media etiquette. I tag publications for this reason when I'm sharing their content.

When you do it closer to home, the benefit is more obvious. As an example: if your friend publishes a great blog post and you share it, use @ again and type that friend's name. This will bring them up as an option to tag in your post, which gives them the opportunity to engage with you or at least thank you for sharing their post.

The first rule you need to keep in mind is that tagging—like most aspects of social media—is all about reciprocity. If you want to draw people to you, you must also draw nearer to others. It's about interaction—the collective versus the self. (That's the *social* bit of social media.) It makes me crazy when a contact tags me in everything they post, but they never once interact with what *I* share. If you treat tagging like a one-way street, don't be surprised to find it's a dead end.

If you insist on tagging people in your posts, do them the courtesy of interacting with their posts, too—whether they tag you or not. I rarely tag anyone because I hate to annoy my community with excessive tagging. (And let's be honest, it really can be annoying.)

If you're promoting a commercial deal, running an event, or selling something, why not drop your contacts a personal note and ask them if they'd be willing to support you rather than tagging them in a post? Personal contact is always better received.

And what about tagging famous (or infamous) people? I'm talking about people who get tagged all the time. I see it in my network constantly—you *can* tag Bill Gates and any number of other big names, but *should* you?

When you want to tag a famous person, think about what they do every day. Do you *really* think they will see what you are sharing? I am sure they have very busy assistants going through their accounts so they can respond to the ones that matter. Put yourself in their shoes. Bill Gates, for example, is trying to solve some of the biggest challenges the world faces. Do you think he has time to respond to everyone tagging him? Is your post worthy of his attention, or are you just trying to call attention to yourself through digital name-dropping?

Indiscriminate tagging is a nightmare for non-celebrities, too. When executives feel overwhelmed by the over-tagging and mindless messages filling their inboxes, they'll quit the very platforms you're trying to attract them on!

In short, think before you tag. If you don't have a *very* good reason to tag someone, especially a public figure, please don't do it. It makes you look silly, it's counter-productive, and it diminishes the effectiveness of LinkedIn as a connectivity platform.

❑ I promise to tag people and businesses appropriately when I share. I'll interact with their posts when I'm tagged I also promise not to tag famous people just for the sake of tagging them.

10 SEND

TWO RECOMMENDATIONS TODAY

Recommendations are important, so you should always seek recommendations for the work you are proud of. We know how precious time is, so when a busy person takes the time to write a recommendation for you, it says a lot about you and your work.

Make a list of the people you want to ask for recommendations. How can you help *them* recommend you? Obviously, you can send a request and hope for the best. But if you outline what they could emphasize and suggest a few things for them to craft into their own language, they're more likely to respond with something pointed and useful. It's natural to feel uncomfortable doing this, but look at it this way: you're making it easy for them to help you (which they want to do) and showing respect for *their* time, which is very important.

The best way to get recommendations is to proactively write recommendations for the people you put on the list you'll make below. Reciprocity makes the world go around. Most people who receive a thoughtful recommendation from you will respond in kind with recommendations. If they need prompting, go to your *edit profile* page, scroll down to the recommendations section, and click on the tab in the right, ***ask to be recommended.***

It's simple, but you must be persistent because this is very important for your career. One effective strategy is to ask people, via some other means, before you send the request on LinkedIn. This small personal gesture will give you a much stronger chance of a response—people really appreciate a little bit of courtesy. If you are looking for a job and really need recommendations, go ahead and mention it. Sometimes you need to light a fire under the people who want to help you. Don't wait for them to act; get on it!

When it comes to people whose recommendations really matter to you, don't be afraid to nag them. It's a big gift we can give when we support each other's careers and ambitions. Make sure you respond in kind to anyone who takes the time to write a recommendation for you. Get out there and recommend as many of your professional connections as you can. They will be delighted to receive a recommendation from you, and we can change the culture of apathy one connection at a time.

Social media is definitely a place where you gain more if you give more. Be a giver! In fact, try to give more recommendations than you get. This will keep you focused on doing it regularly.

Notes—people I want to recommend and people I'd love a recommendation from:

_____

_____

_____

_____

❑ **I've written and sent two recommendations.** It's good to give!

11 LIST YOUR SKILLS

If you haven't already done this, add a list of your skills on LinkedIn. Under your *edit profile* section, click on the **add skills** button. You can add up to 50 skills—and the best bit is that a window drops down with suggestions of skills you might add. If you enter "marketing," it will give you every variation of marketing you could list, thus making it very easy to get to 50. But should you really list 50 skills?

Before we discuss how many skills you should list, you might be wondering how important the LinkedIn **skills section is in the first place. Well, it's important to** know that recruiters now have the option of searching for and narrowing down candidates by their skills—LinkedIn skills, that is. So, this section is only going to become more important.

If you don't have a *skills* section:

1. Click on your profile—a simple click on your photo will take you there

2. Then *view profile*

3. Click *add profile section*

4. Click *core* and select *add skills* from the dropdown

5. In the *add skills* pop-up window, start selecting your skills

6. Remember to place the top three skills you want to be endorsed for on top

7. Don't forget to save

While you are in the *skills* section, click on the three dots:

Figure 41. Look for the skill quiz

Then click on *endorsement settings*—this is a relatively new feature on LinkedIn. If you want to give and to provide endorsements, make sure all toggles are on *yes*!

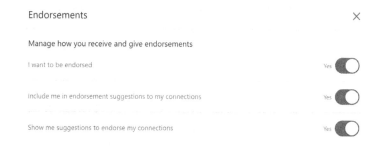

Figure 42. Find endorsements

Today LinkedIn skills do not always appear when you view someone's profile. If you want to endorse someone's skills, click on their profile, go to the *skills* section, and simply endorse them for the skills you value.

If you're set up to endorse others (third in the list above) when a skills endorsement window appears while you're on LinkedIn, or on their profile, all you need to do is click endorse and it's done. There was a more complicated process, but it seems LinkedIn is back to making this section simple.

Once you endorse someone, this appears on their profile, and it's the easiest way for any of us to provide a recommendation for a colleague or someone we admire.

Our goal in our *skills* section is to get core skills endorsed 99+ times, and that means you'll have a strong ranking for that skill in the big SEO database of LinkedIn. These are the skills that have a true impact. Therefore, keep your eye on your skills section, making it your goal to get core skills endorsed over 99+ times, and then you will rank higher in searches for people with these skills.

The best strategy is to select your top three skills, which you sit at the top of your skills section. You can re-order your skills by clicking the three dots again.

$$\left(\ \text{Take skill quiz}\ \right)\quad \cdots\quad +$$

Figure 43. Use the dots to reorder skills

Once any skill reaches 99+, move it down and move another important skill into the top three. Viewers on your profile initially see only the first three, which is why you make sure it's at the top.

Your highest-ranked skills demonstrate to interested parties (including recruiters) that this is an area of expertise for you. If you're too lazy to write recommendations—and *admit it, some of you* are—this is the next best thing. Endorse those skills when they pop up and help your friends, peers, and community be more successful. But make sure you have your key skills on top as well.

Finally, here's a really important job for anyone who updated their LinkedIn skills years ago and has never been back to check. Review the skills you have listed and ask yourself: are they outdated? Can you delete some?

Any skills with 99+ endorsements are probably worth keeping, but when it comes to those skills that are no longer relevant or have landed you few endorsements, consider deleting them.

You can have 50 skills, but if you want to get 99+ endorsements on your key skills, I recommend only having 10 to choose from. Slim it down, make it more high-level, be strategic in this section, and then when all 10 get to 99+ endorsements, add some new ones and start again.

Don't forget, the best way to get people ticking *yes* to your skills is to tick those skills for others when they pop up, or actively seek them out on their profiles. Remember what we said about reciprocity? Get on it.

Notes—skills I want to profile:

_____

_____

_____

_____

_____

❑ **I've looked at five other people whom I know and endorsed their skills.** It's good to give!

12 ARE YOU LOOKING FOR A JOB?

You'll get the most out of LinkedIn if you help LinkedIn help you. When you are in your own profile, under your photo, name, summary, and more, you'll see three sections—click on *open to*. This is for job seekers and for those hiring.

If you're open to finding a new job, click on this and you have a space to fill in your preferences. These include where you live and the cities where you are interested in working, the type of job or job title, how you want to work, whether it appears on your profile, etc. One way you make LinkedIn work for you is by giving it as much information as you can to ensure it is feeding you with the best roles available. If I was looking for work, this is the first thing I would do.

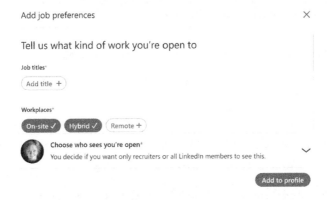

Figure 44. Be clear about your job preferences

Remember to click through to **choose who sees you're open** at the bottom of this form. It can be all of LinkedIn or only recruiters. If you work for a company and don't want your boss to know you're looking elsewhere, click on only recruiters. Note: recruiters that work for your company will not see this alert.

Choose who sees you're open*
You decide if you want only recruiters or all LinkedIn members to see this. ⌄

Figure 45. You can choose who sees you're open

In August 2016, LinkedIn launched its **Open Candidates** mode, which then changed to **Open to Work.** According to LinkedIn, turning on *open to work* doubles the likelihood of getting a message from a recruiter. Depending on whether it's public or private, those who can see it will see the green frame around your profile picture with #OpenToWork.

I also recommend upgrading to a **Premium Career** (previously Job Seeker Premium) subscription if you are serious about looking for work. The first month is free, and when you are looking for a new job, the additional cost is an investment worth making. Get organized before signing up for the free 30-day trial and you might be able to make the most of it before being obligated to pay.

Premium Career gives you four critical things:

1. Insights into the applications you've submitted and where you stand

2. More information on who is viewing your profile, which is a chance to know if you are generating interest, and whose attention you're attracting

3. Access to on-demand learning—and this is now a massive resource. When you do these courses, you

can also add them to your LinkedIn profile, which is a strong sign to potential employers

4. And finally, my least favorite tool on LinkedIn: InMail. In a job-searching situation, this is incredibly valuable.

I'll have more to say about general Premium later.

Some other tips if you're on the hunt for a job:

- Start with LinkedIn's job board. Recommendations based on your profile will appear in the right-hand column of your profile all the time but go straight to linkedin.com/jobs/ and more personalized recommendations will appear. When you click on this, on the left-hand side is a list of options and helpful tools you can explore.

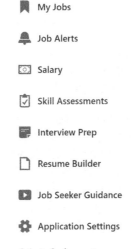

Figure 46. Job-hunting support

- Search by skills—we talked about skills above, so searching for jobs linked to specific skills is a great opportunity. Say "operation manager" (jobs will be a suggestion, as will groups, etc.) and if you click on jobs, it will take you to the options. Check out this link for more information on how you can find work with your skills linkedin.github.io/career-explorer/.

- Search remote jobs. If you want a remote job, search with the title of the job you'd like and the word "remote."

- Hashtags are a boon for the job seeker! People who post jobs on LinkedIn are more likely to use hashtags to make them easier to find. Sometimes the hashtags are general, such as #hiringnow #nowhiring #jobs #applytoday #openrecruitment #joinourteam. Others may be specific, like #HiringSocialMedia. Some examples I found using this hashtag include: #socialmedia #hiringsocialmedia #hiring #hiringnow #hiringimmediately #remotework #socialmediajobs #communitymanagement #recruiting #jobopportunities #marketing #digitalmarketing.

- Track what people are posting on LinkedIn, as well as in groups.

- Follow recruiters in your field on LinkedIn. Keep an eye on what they're posting.

And your alumni and networking connections are also people you can reach out to. Hint: help others, and when your time comes, more help with be offered. Always thank anyone who did anything for you too. In the recruitment and job seeker area on LinkedIn, there are always new developments to keep an eye out for. Stay up to date on what is happening, because it is a fabulous platform to help you get where you want to be.

Though LinkedIn is so much more than a recruitment tool, that aspect of it remains a critical core strength of the platform. If you are looking for a new job, make sure you use LinkedIn to its full potential.

Hot Tip #3!

There's been talk that you can gift your first-degree connections a free three-month subscription to *LinkedIn Premium*. The goal is to help them in the job search—how's that for #GivingEconomy? Look in the *Premium* area of your profile.

Let's make sure we are using this to help our community during these challenging years for everyone.

13 USE LINKEDIN GROUPS

LinkedIn Groups are a terrific resource that you should not ignore. You can join up to 100 groups; however, it is impossible to participate actively and intelligently across all of them, so be selective! I recommend choosing a maximum of 10 that are relevant to you. And even then, if you can participate effectively in more than three, you obviously have too much time on your hands :-).

When you're deciding which groups to join, go to the *groups* tab, and search for groups aligned to your profession. You'll find the *groups* tab under the *work* button at the top, right-hand side of your LinkedIn profile page. It looks like this.

Work ▼

Figure 47. Groups are in *work*

Another easy way to find groups is to enter "groups" in the LinkedIn search window and click on the link that appears. This search will also give you recommendations for groups aligned to your profile, which can be very handy for finding relevant ones to join.

As a best practice, I recommend focusing on groups organized according to three themes:

1. Geographic: people near you

2. Specific position: people who have the same job as you

3. Industry: people in your industry

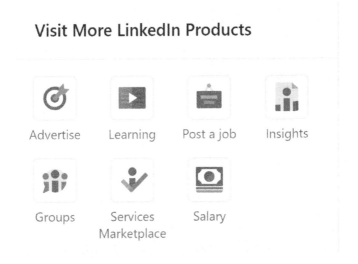

Figure 48. Finding Groups in *more LinkedIn products*

When you join groups, you can indicate how often you want to be notified of group activities. For groups in which you want to be really engaged, tick the daily email, but *for the rest, tick the weekly email* or the no email notification at all option. The more groups you join, the more overwhelming these emails can be. Group posts now appear in your LinkedIn feed, a recent change that I believe helps encourage more participation.

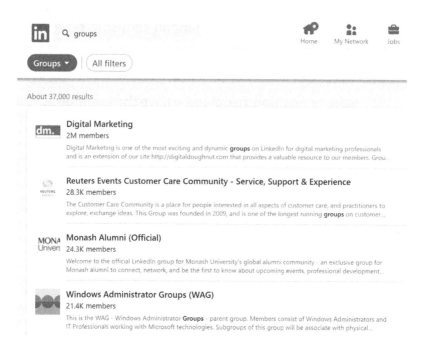

Figure 49. Search for "groups"

Another option to **find the right groups** is to ask your peers, customers, partners, and other influencers in your field where they are. What groups do they value? Where do they get the best insights? All group activity is now private, so you can only see what is going on in a group after you have joined. It's hard to gauge what is valuable in advance, so asking around is a way to save you time and get you to the most relevant groups for your profession.

Once you've joined a group, **carefully monitor it**, and see how other members are participating. Some people will advise you to blast all your groups with information, such as your blog posts. I completely disagree with this strategy. Sure, you can build a profile by getting your name out there, but at what cost to your credibility? For many people, including the executives I work with, aggressive self-promotion is fundamentally against what effective, meaningful social leadership is all about. If you want to win hearts and minds, be very careful about annoying your audience—even when you see other people doing it.

So, **go easy on the self-promotion.** A more subtle way to get your content out there is to find a buddy (or a team of buddies) who promote your work, and you post theirs to return the favor.

How useful are LinkedIn Groups, really?

Once you've started using and participating in various groups, you can be your own judge of their usefulness for you. Many people find them to be too spammy, depending on how participants in their groups operate and self-promote.

Group updates appearing in your feed, as I mentioned above, is a promising new development, but at the time of this writing, LinkedIn Groups is still not an ideal experience. I'm part of more professional groups on Facebook, where I find the simpler model and notification system easier to manage.

With that said, some industries, such as construction, energy, and gas, operate almost exclusively through LinkedIn Groups. Real business is happening there daily. It's important to understand the power of LinkedIn Groups for *your* industry. If that's where the action is happening, that's where you need to be. There is no one-size-fits-all approach to LinkedIn Groups, and you can certainly make the best of the ones where you choose to participate.

Notes—types of groups I want to join:

_____

_____

_____

_____

_____

❑ **I've applied to three groups.**

14 LIST
THE CAUSES YOU CARE ABOUT AND PROMOTE THE ONES YOU VOLUNTEER FOR

LinkedIn gives you the option, when you're building your profile, to list the causes you volunteer for and care about. This is a small section, but do spend some time on it. Even if you are not actively participating in any causes, you can still list what you care about. This gives future customers, partners, employees, and employers insight into the sort of person you are.

You've already noticed that many people are on social media to promote themselves, sell products, or just bore the pants off everyone around them. But great social media participation is much more than that, and a lot of being a meaningful leader, regardless of the platform, comes down to what you give to your audience. You share great information because you think the people who follow you will value it. You create great content so you can share the things you are learning or experiencing. This is the fundamental power of social media.

It's about our collective humanity—which means that small things like the volunteer experience and the causes section are important to share, and I recommend spending the time to make this section of your LinkedIn profile as strong as any other.

We bring our whole self to work today. This is part of owning that.

Causes

Animal Welfare • Arts and Culture • Children • Civil Rights and Social Action • Disaster and Humanitarian Relief • Economic Empowerment • Education • Environment • Human Rights • Poverty Alleviation • Politics • Social Services Veteran Support

Figure 50. Your causes and volunteering

Notes—my causes and volunteering over the years:

_____

_____

_____

_____

_____

❑ **I've added these to my LinkedIn profile.**

15 HAVE YOU BEEN PUBLISHED ANYWHERE?

Under the *Publications* section in your profile, you can add any content you've created and published somewhere else. If you have been published anywhere beyond your blog (academic papers, whitepapers, books, ebooks, guest articles, etc.) include these to help build a complete profile of who you are, what you stand for, and what you've achieved.

LinkedIn has changed dramatically over the years and there are many ways to feature your published work. Adding it here is a simple process and adds weight to your overall profile. The more sections you fill out on LinkedIn, the greater the chance to get to all-star status.

The published section appears under your accomplishments, and looks like this:

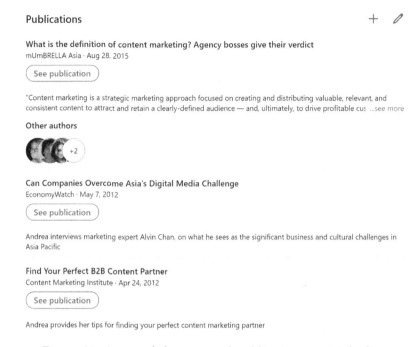

Figure 51. Accomplishments and publications on LinkedIn

Under **add to profile** you'll find other possibilities, like adding patents, projects, volunteer experience, and more. Click on these and see what else you can add to make your profile outstanding!

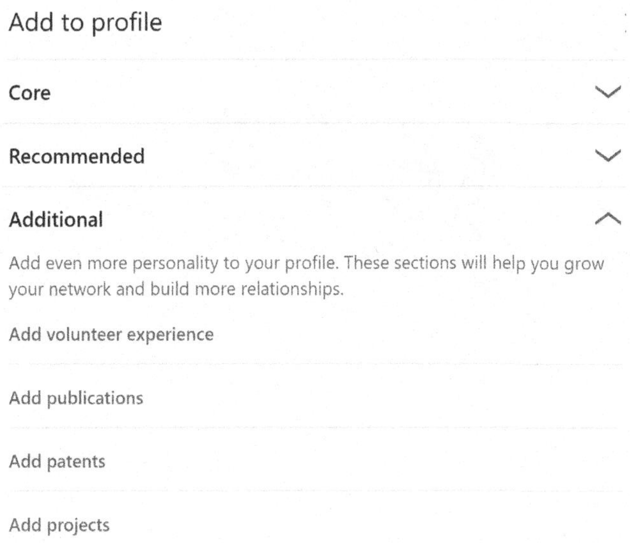

Add to profile

Core ⌄

Recommended ⌄

Additional ⌃

Add even more personality to your profile. These sections will help you grow
your network and build more relationships.

Add volunteer experience

Add publications

Add patents

Add projects

Figure 52. More about the whole you

Notes—I've been published in:

_____

_____

_____

_____

_____

❏ **I've added these to my profile.**

16 ADD
HONORS, AWARDS, AND ASSOCIATIONS

What **awards and recognition have your achievements earned you?** Even if you are at the beginning of your career, look to your past and find what is valuable to mention in this section. These can be global awards or more local recognition. Whatever you have been recognized for, make sure it is linked to your professional profile—these things matter. Also, don't forget that internal awards are great to include as well. Keep this section updated as the awards flow in.

Additionally, what **professional associations** are you involved in? Make sure you list any professional associations as you join them, and if the association is on LinkedIn, you can link your profile to it. If you are on an executive committee or have a non-executive role, list it. Anyone who has been part of an association knows and respects what a commitment this entails. Make sure you let your audience know about it. This section is primarily for professional pursuits, but if you are a member of charitable associations, include them here, too.

Notes—list of my associations:

_____

_____

_____

_____

List of my awards:

_____

_____

_____

_____

❑   **I've added both to my profile.**

17 Go PREMIUM

Let's talk about whether you should pay for a Premium membership, especially if your company doesn't offer it to you. In my experience, few companies offer Premium subscriptions to their employees. Typically, only people in sales benefit from paid services like Sales Navigator.

This is a huge missed opportunity because paid accounts empower employees to dig deeper on LinkedIn. In today's world, virtually everyone is in sales and marketing, and the idea that only certain employees get access to the best tools is something that needs to change. The challenge is that companies often still believe that only salespeople touch the customer, something we know is not true. Companies should invest in and encourage employees who are engaged on LinkedIn by paying for Premium membership.

In the meantime, basic LinkedIn is free, but consider upgrading to Premium membership. Here are a few benefits of being a Premium member:

- A Premium membership means you appear higher in searches when people are looking for professionals with your skills.

- You can find more people.

- Your profile is more visible.

- Apart from people who appear anonymously **(don't be one of those people),** you can see more information on who has been viewing your profile.

- When you are prospecting for new business leads, you have more criteria options with which to search.

- Premium membership gives you InMail access, which means you can connect and exchange with people who are not your first-degree connections.

In addition to all of the above, investing in yourself through a Premium upgrade demonstrates that you take the platform seriously—an essential consideration if you want to make the most of what LinkedIn can do for your career.

If you want to consider going Premium, you can find more information here premium.linkedin.com. Keep in mind: when you use a service for free, you are paying with your data.

I pay for LinkedIn because I do not want to be the product. In fact, I pay for services whenever I can for this very reason. If we had subscription models across all social media, we might be closer to solving many of the challenges we currently face. For some reason, that conversation doesn't seem to be happening at all.

❏ **I'm Premium**

18 FINAL TIPS ON LINKEDIN

If you do everything I've suggested so far, you're going to have an impressive and effective profile—we're aiming for **all-star, right?** However, don't think you can do it once, tick that box, and move on.

Keep going back to refresh images or links to content and update your content regularly. The internet is dynamic and always evolving. Static is stagnant, and your LinkedIn profile should be never be stagnant.

Equally, LinkedIn is in a state of never-ending evolution, to ensure it delivers excellent experiences for us, the users. As I was writing updates to this book, the whole look and feel of LinkedIn changed—again! I am happy with the changes, which isn't always the case.

LinkedIn is never going to get everything right, but overall, I feel that is doing its best to be the best professional platform in the world. Not every change is worthy of this update, but I've gone wide and deep to capture as much as I can about the changes that matter.

Some additional suggestions for a dynamic profile:

- Make sure your education information is up to date and link your learning institution to your profile. If a school still exists and has a LinkedIn page, it will come up as a linking option.

- If you work on a **major project** with a team of people (and it isn't a top-secret), add the title of the project with a quick summary and link to the profiles of team members involved in the project. This means the project description will appear on their profiles too, and it's a powerful way to connect professionals to each other.

- LinkedIn lets you provide advice on **making contact** with you. My profile says: "Make sure it's appropriate, and if you want to pitch something to me, tell me why you've targeted me in the first instance. I'll read it if you can justify why you thought I'd be a good contact." Most people ignore this kind of disclaimer, but it's important to be proactive about the kind of communication you want.

- Listing **languages** in which you are proficient is a must!

- LinkedIn's **video features**—including live video—are an effective way to promote your thought leadership or the work you are doing. Remember, if you post an original video (under 10 minutes) directly onto LinkedIn, the platform will provide more support for that content than if it's a link to something you posted elsewhere, such as on YouTube. I alternate between posting directly and sharing a link to YouTube.

- LinkedIn **live audio events**—think Clubhouse for LinkedIn—are being rolled out as I write this. Live video events too. This is an area to keep an eye on, but remember, just because it's new doesn't mean it's good for your audience. Some people LOVE this stuff, and some couldn't think of anything worse. While Clubhouse didn't work for me, I'll keep an open mind about this feature on LinkedIn.

- Keep an eye on **creator mode**, with new changes coming, including more audio opportunities. LinkedIn creator mode is all about increasing audiences, engagement, and content visibility, so if you are publishing content, pay attention to how it's evolving. It also emphasizes following versus connecting. Building followers versus connections is a great move.

- Do not **share content** onto LinkedIn from an external platform such as Hootsuite, Buffer, or an employee advocacy platform. Share directly onto LinkedIn, or you will be punished by LinkedIn through fewer views. It also impacts your SSI score.

- Keep an eye out for **LinkedIn themes** and participate in the ones that resonate. As a content platform, LinkedIn always features current and trending content. To keep up to date, follow LinkedIn's company pages, and follow LinkedIn's editors. Two trends kicking of 2022 were #2022goals and #VisionBoardDay. In 2021 we had moments like #ThisLittleGirlIsme too. What is something you want to be part of?

- Finally, always be looking **for new updates** to LinkedIn. This powerful platform is a constant work in progress and great new options are constantly being developed.

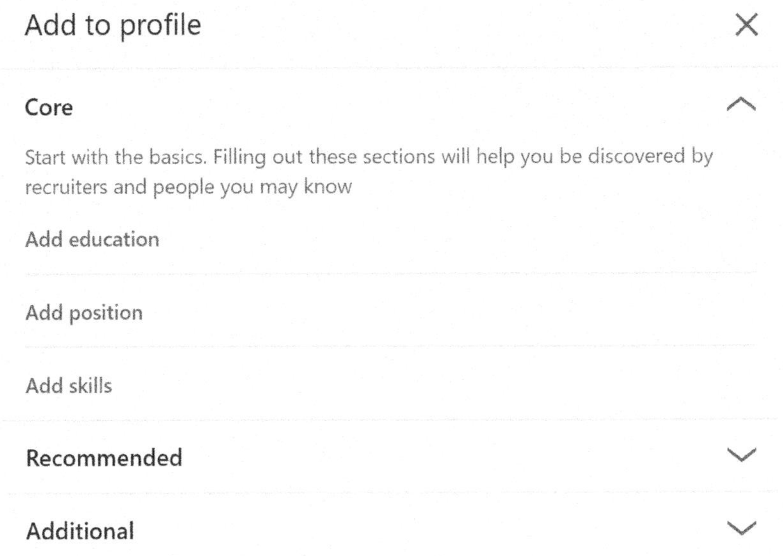

Add to profile   ✕

Core   ⌃

Start with the basics. Filling out these sections will help you be discovered by recruiters and people you may know

Add education
_____

Add position
_____

Add skills

Recommended   ⌄
_____

Additional   ⌄

Figure 53. Adding more sections to your profile

❑ I've looked at the addition sections and added the ones relevant to me now.

Be Amazing

Using social media as an all-star pro is about sharing your knowledge and passion with your community—no matter your topic or focus. There is an audience for every subject, after all. The important attitude is to remember that it's more about what you give than what you get. Becoming a powerful social leader is an **act of service.** How can you serve your community and make it better, smarter, and more successful? It's not about you. **It's never been about you,** and that is a message any social media cynic (you know who you are) can appreciate.

Don't throw the baby out with that bathwater, even if you've been turned off by self-promoting behavior on social media. We are all competing globally today, and the fact that the loudest voices can drown out many quieter, more valuable voices is a defining challenge of our time. Be a part of the solution by building a strong social leadership position as an act of service, versus the self-serving approach more common today. It's a fine line understanding the difference. However, if you can embrace the idea of service as central to your social leadership presence, we'll all be one step closer to making our corporate online world a more positively connected and empowering place.

Engaging in a global platform and giving of yourself in this way—and doing it well—means you will receive so much in return: professional opportunities, new communities, speaking invitations, new customers, personal growth opportunities, trust, loyalty, and the feeling of impacting many lives for the better.

It's critical to be a positive force on social media. Disagreeing with someone is fine but be constructive in your criticism and always be open to opposing views. Have a conversation, not an argument. No one wins a social media argument, anyway. Don't feed the trolls!

It's important to participate by supporting and celebrating others in your field. However, be very wary of overdoing your participation. On LinkedIn in particular, people *switch off from* connections who are annoyingly overactive. We are asking our audience for too much time invested in us. And with the dearth of information available, it is hard to get that much time from people. Do less and be awesome, especially now. Participation on LinkedIn has increased since 2020. Less is always better.

I recommend posting no more than once a day (or once a week or month—consistency is what matters). Your time is very valuable, and not over-posting should help you manage how much time you spend on social media. It is more effective to show up less often in your contacts' news feeds but to be world-class every time you do.

When you share your own content (blogs, videos, etc.) you are asking your audience to do you a favor—to give you their time. When you share other people's content that's aligned to the topics you care most about, you are doing your audience a favor—finding valuable, world-class information for them so they don't have to find it themselves. Our goal, as social leaders, is to become a one-stop shop in our area of expertise. Spend most of your social media time sharing quality content from other people and participating meaningfully in conversations. Contribute this way, and occasionally ask for your followers' time with your own content. They will not mind giving it to you when you have served them so well.

We've reached a point of content shock and saturation today. Social media should never be used as a megaphone for your views. If you want to be heard at all, aim to be excellent by adding value, lifting people up, engaging in discussions, and boosting your community to make everyone a champion.

It's also critical to focus on earning people's respect and trust, but you must be patient. It really can take a long time to build your profile and credibility, especially if you are still coming up through the ranks of your profession.

Finally, be critical of the advice you get—and that even goes for what I am writing here. If it doesn't resonate with you and who *you* are, find your own way. There is no one right way to be successful on social media or LinkedIn. Listen to others but listen to yourself first and trust your own judgment—it's rarely wrong when you really listen to it.

Things You Can Do
to Keep Lifting Your
Profile

The steps I've outlined are a starting point in helping you become successful on LinkedIn by creating a compelling profile. They will also get you to All-Star. If you implement these 18 things now, it will help you establish your presence and become confident in your participation. These are only some of the things I've learned, and LinkedIn is changing all the time. I've invested deeply in various social platforms and blogs over more than a decade, and these recommendations come from working with thousands of professionals on their social leadership skills. The first question I always get is *where do I start?* Start with the 18 points we've discussed, then consider my eight final steps below. See these as a bonus!

Eight more things for the over-achievers:

1. **Define who you are** and **what you want to be known for**. Tie your social voice to your heart and mind, and get your focus clear, because this is how you make an impact and build a strong social leadership position. If you don't know where to start, ask the people closest to you: *What am I good at? What is my passion? What makes me stand out in a crowd? What is my gift to the world?*

2. **Define your social channels**, starting with LinkedIn if you are a professional. Make sure you have complete profiles across all channels. It takes time to do a great job at this. Which channels should you use? The simple rule is, you should be where your customers are— but you should also be on social media platforms *you* enjoy. This is critical. Keep in mind you can learn to enjoy them over time, too. I hated Twitter when I started, and now I love it. But for all professionals, LinkedIn is a must.

3. **Identify the content resources you can rely on** for knowledge and inspiration today (*Harvard Business Review*, the *New York Times*, BBC, TED Talks, the *Guardian*, your business content, etc.) and then make a commitment to share one article, video, or audio a week—everyone can do that! If you loved something or it inspired you, don't you think someone else would value it too? When you share any information, always add your opinion to the post. This is where you deliver value to your audience. Sharing content without offering a nugget of interpretation is a wasted opportunity. People are looking to cut through the noise of social media and to overcome the content shock, so you can help them do that by guiding them to your content through your words. This is called microblogging.

4. **Start creating your own content.** Is blogging in you? If you decide to blog, Get started by publishing articles on LinkedIn, and then build your own blogging platform (using WordPress, for example). Maybe video is your thing (launch a YouTube channel), or podcasting? Once you know you're committed to content creation, why not launch your own professional website? If you're not sure what to talk about when you begin creating your own content, start by answering the questions

you get asked the most and add a unique layer of insight in your answers—something that no one else is talking about. Once you start, you will be amazed at how the ideas for future content will flow through you.

5. **Another new content opportunity** is LinkedIn's new newsletter feature. You can build a subscriber base there. However, I suggest prioritizing your own platforms (a website or newsletter tool) rather than publishing everything on a platform (like LinkedIn) because you do not own it. Don't forget, if a platform closes down, you will lose everything you've uploaded there. And if you think LinkedIn is too big to fail, the members in mainland China might have some insight for you. On October 14th, 2021, LinkedIn announced it would shut down its service in mainland China.

6. **Don't think about what you will get; focus on giving and supporting** as the priority. Give, give, give to receive, and the wins will come. In a social media context, joining the Giving Economy means that you become a social leader by focusing your attention on helping others be successful as a bigger priority. You will feel good, and it adds tremendous meaning to your presence. It's also the fastest way to build your social leadership profile, by being a champion of your community. The people who succeed the most are driven to create change in their field. It is this drive that ensures success, not how you compare to anyone else. What change do you want to see in the world? Become a voice for that change and be part of the #GivingEconomy.

7. **Be unique.** Following the crowd is a common phenomenon across all social media platforms. People who have succeeded with certain styles of video are

copied by everyone. Blogs, imagery, everything, there is a lot of 'sameness' going on. Be inspired by others but find your own path. One new feature on LinkedIn, for example, is surveys, and it seems that everyone is doing them, constantly. While there is value in the surveys, when everyone is doing the same thing, do you want to join the crowd—or continue to shine in your own, unique way?

8. **Be brave enough to make mistakes**, get stuck in, find your way, work it out, learn, grow, and excel. Some people are intimidated by social media. If you define your story, define your audience, then define the social media channels best suited to sharing your story and the content and opinions you want to be known for, you will already be miles ahead of many others in your field. It's hard putting yourself out there—I know this from experience. So prepare yourself, have a goal, and get started. Then evolve as you go. Define what success means for *you*, then chart your own unique path to get there.

Thank you so much for reading this book. I am incredibly passionate about the opportunity we all have, through social leadership, to fundamentally shift our world for the better.

Set aside your limiting beliefs and take this chance to be a powerful and positive force on social media. We need your voice and your vision, so it's time to step up and be excellent.

Cheers,

Andrea

PS: keep reading for a brief introduction to the concept I'm calling the Social Leadership Manifesto. One day it will be a book, but for now, let it sink in and inspire you to step into more meaningful participation.

The Social Leadership Manifesto
Are you ready to take your place?

In an age of distrust

Social media is a mess. It has become a destructive and divisive force in our societies, and its incredible potential has been squandered by bad actors. Social media companies appear to lack the willingness to take full responsibility for the problems this has created, even when war is being raged on these platforms. Profits at the expense of humanity are on display for all to see.

Social media companies rank way down at the bottom of our trust, as far as news sources go. Distrust is now our default emotion, unfortunately.

NEWS SOURCES FAIL TO FIX THEIR TRUST PROBLEM

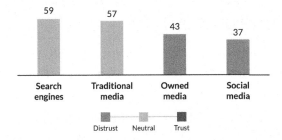

Source: Edelman Trust Barometer 2022

This is a depressing reality when we have so many complex issues to overcome in the world. When you have little trust, life is less. When you have little trust, the global challenges facing us in the 2020s seem more impossible to overcome. It is little wonder mental health issues are reaching unprecedented levels in modern times.

The truth of this moment in time is people are running out of hope. Hopelessness is destructive, and as a result, we are being consumed by cynicism or inaction. As leaders, we need to show people that hope is the way forward, otherwise, we let those who have been trying to divide us win.

> *'Distrust is now our default emotion, with nearly 60 percent of people inclined towards distrust'*
> —Edelman

We also must be willing to confront the idea that the tools of our time—social media in this case—is 100% responsible for the challenges we face. What is happening has happened before throughout history, and we didn't have social media then. While the tools are part of the problem, the essential truth is WE are the problem, the societies we have built are the problem, and it's long overdue we address that.

Today, social media is where it is happening, but I do not believe it's the root cause. It doesn't mean we can't correct what is happening on social media, and in the wider world.

Where do we go from here?

In the age of distrust, business is a surprisingly critical player in reducing disinformation and division. Edelman's Trust Barometer lays out the situation:[18]

"We are looking towards business leaders to get us out of the multiple global crises we face, with CEOs and the businesses they represent seen as not doing enough for

---

18 https://www.edelman.com/trust/2022-trust-barometer

climate change (52%), economic inequality (49%), workforce reskilling (46%) and trustworthy information (42%)."

The role of leadership now is to speak up on the biggest issues that matter. This means having views and taking action on climate change, discrimination, and inequity. In other words, these challenges call for social leadership.

Business needs a world of social prosperity in order to function. But beyond profits, beyond business as usual, we must take a stand for humanity, meet our challenges head on, and work together to overcome them. It won't be simple, it won't be fast, and everyone needs to get involved.

You can and do make a difference

We all have the power to make a positive difference when we claim our space in the digital world. Social leadership is a role all employees can and must embrace. This mindset is not happening in businesses today. They are not unleashing their people. But here's the truth—it is not only business leaders whose voice is valuable today—in fact, your coworkers may trust you more than they do your CEO or your government leaders. People trust people they know, and they trust authentic leaders.

Data: Edelman Trust Barometer 2022

Some business leaders, who do not trust employees to represent the company in accordance with company rules or values, may push back on employees speaking up on social media. However, employees speak to customers, partners, and all other stakeholders daily. Trusting them and empowering them to step into their voice on social media is empowering for everyone. It is good for business too.

Rather than discouraging social media participation, train and support your team to excel at it. Help them shine, and you will build an army of advocates for your business who will transform it from the inside out.

The Social Leadership Manifesto

A manifesto is a declaration of core values and beliefs that functions both as a statement of principle and as a call to action. Your manifesto won't look exactly like mine, but I recommend you craft your social leadership presence around the following four categories:

- Who I am
- Action taker
- Committed to mastery
- What I give

Here are some of the elements within each of these categories to get you started on your Social Leadership journey.

Who I Am

A social leader is...

- **Respectful** – social leaders appreciate the complexity and diversity of the digital world. They give respect and demand respect in return, for themselves and their community.

- **Authentic** – this is the pixie dust of social leadership. They are in tune with the inner truth of who they are, and all that they stand for. They participate in alignment with their values.

- **Humble** – they know no one person alive has all the answers. They are humble before that essential truth.

- And more.

Action Taker

An active social leader is...

- **Focused** – they stand for something meaningful to them, with a strong and clear voice. They are clear on the reason why they show up as a social leader.

- **Engaged in conversation** – while putting their own point of view out there is important, they see engaging with their community is even more important.

- **Troll-smart** – they can spot a troll, bully, or bot anywhere and they do not engage. They do not let them get under their skin. They will never let a troll silence their voice.

- And more.

A bonus for social leaders who are employees:

- **In alignment with company values** – when they are employed by a company, they know their obligation is to participate in alignment with the company's core values. Companies are not a democracy.

Committed to Mastery

A social leader is committed to mastery...

- **Storytelling** – they know stories run the world. It is the language of legends, business, and success. A social leader embraces the mindset of a storyteller and masters the skill.

- **Delivering world-class content** – their own and others.

  - **Their own** – they are not afraid to put their thought leadership out into the world. They see content creation as an investment in themselves as it helps them master their own knowledge.

  - **Others aligned to their voice** – they seek others in their area of expertise, actively sharing their powerful and impactful thought leadership. They are committed to giving their audience access to wider perspectives.

- **Audience focused** – they are clear on the audience they are speaking to. They are strongly empathetic and can easily put themselves in the shoes of their audience.

- **Steadfastly verifying information** – they work hard to ensure they never share misinformation. They check multiple sources. They seek to verify and take that extra step of cross-checking before sharing. They respect experts.

- And more.

What I give

A social leader's gift to the world is...

- **Inspiring** – they know their role in delivering hope to a bruised world. They are part of the movement to rebuild trust, and ready to inspire their audience, creating ripples of change.

- **Earning the right to their audience's time** – they appreciate the value of attention and take the role seriously, understanding anything they produce or share must be worth their audience's time.

- **Courage** – to step fully into their power, their heart beats with great courage. They know the reason for being there is more important than any fear that could hold them back.

- And more.

For access to *The Social Leadership Manifesto*, simply scan this code.

SCAN ME

Are you ready to lead?

It is time for people like you and me to step up and bring the digital conversation back in balance. Are you ready to join us in redirecting the world towards the priorities we must face together?

Together, by following the principles in The Social Leadership Manifesto, we can achieve what many claim is impossible. But it's the hope our world is looking for, because when you look around, you can see that our collective future is at stake. Are you ready to take your place at this important moment for humanity? Are you ready to lead and be a social leader? Let's go.

Andrea T Edwards, CSP

Andrea T Edwards CSP is the Digital Conversationalist. She is a globally award-winning B2B communications professional with over 20 years of experience. Recognised by the Book Authority as one of the best LinkedIn books of all times, Andrea is the author of Uncommon Courage, she hosts the Know Show weekly and speaks on social leadership, courage and how to apply the Social Leadership Manifesto in your organization. Andrea is a change agent, provocateur, author, passionate communicator, and social leader.

18 Steps to an All-Star LinkedIn Profile, Andrea's book first published in 2020, received Book Authority's listings on the "100 Best LinkedIn Books of All Time" and "22 Best New LinkedIn eBooks to Read In 2021," and then again in 2022.

Andrea's more recent book, *Uncommon Courage: an Invitation,* hopes to inspire conversations that change the direction of how we live. It's an invitation to be your courageous best self every day. It's also an antidote to the overwhelm, fear, and rage rolling around the world. Uncommon Courage opens a path to inner contentment, peace, and happiness through meaningful action. It brings you an opportunity to reflect: what if there was another way? What if we could do something about the bigger issues facing our world? What if we could make meaningful change? Well, we can—and she lays it out.

You can join Andrea for more insights with special guests on her podcast *Uncommon Courage* and her weekly livestream *The Know Show* with Tim Wade, Joe Augustin, and special guests every week. You can find her on social media @AndreaTEdwards, or visit her websites: www.andreatedwards.com and www.Uncommon-Courage.com.

Acknowledgments

A book like this is based on passion and uncompromising belief in your ideas combined with decades of experience through a lot of ups and downs! My thanks to the leaders in Microsoft, IBM, BNP Paribas Securities Services, and many more for trusting me, taking a risk with these ideas, and partnering with me to prove that social leadership is a powerful tool for business transformation and can deliver huge results for any business professional. You have all helped me hone these ideas into the 18 steps I've outlined in this book.

Many thanks to Stanimira Koleva (my first executive champion), Tiffani Bova, Nishan Weerasinghe, Michelle Cockrill, Julian Kasparian, Wendy McEwan, Sinisa Nikolic, Thariyan Chacko, Shalaka Verma, Eric Schnatterly, Deepthi Anne, James Taylor, Andrew Bryant, Jerome Joseph, Pamela Wigglesworth, Kevin Cottam, John Gordon, Lindsay Adams, Warwick Merry, Kerrie Phipps, Cathy Johnson, Karen Leong, and Natalie Turner—legends all. An extra shout-out to Anne Phey, Sunny Panjabi, and Tara Cremin-Moody too. You three have been amazing supporters of my work. Thanks as well to Natasha David for her early editing work.

I definitely wouldn't have gotten this book across the line without Joanne Flinn whose Authority Services got my book strategy clear and pulled together over a hundred pieces—in record swift time. Thanks so much, Joanne, you amazing professional, for taking the pressure of a book not done off my back. Now it's live and helping people unleash their voices. The truth is, we need the humble, the introspective, the intelligent, the passionate, and the givers to step into their voices. When this happens, we can collectively make the world a better place!

I want to thank one of the most important women in my life, Vicky Minguillo, aka Aunty Vick. Not only did you teach me how to be a better mother, but you've given me the most valuable gift to chase my dreams—time. I love and honor you, sister from another mother.

Finally, a huge thanks to the men in my life. My husband Steve Johnson—you believed in me while enduring the journey (during which I wasn't always pleasant to be around) and never wavered in your support for me though you didn't always agree with how I wanted to go about things. You are perfect for me. And thanks to my boys, Lex and Jax. You let me travel for my work without making me feel too guilty about it, and I've got to tell you, it's the cutest thing watching you look at my YouTube channel. I know what I talk about is boring for you, maybe one day, you'll understand what it was all about.

Love youse all! xxxx